SUBURBANISM

POETICS

Robert Wood is interested in belonging, social relations, and ecology. He is the author of *History & The Poet*, a frequent contributor to the *Los Angeles Review of Books*, and has held fellowships at a number of Ivy League Universities. His archive is housed at the Kislak Special Collections Library at the University of Pennsylvania. Robert currently teaches at the University of Western Australia, is Chair of PEN Perth, and works at The Centre for Stories. He grew up in the suburb of Wembley.

SUBURBANISM

POETICS

ROBERT WOOD

Australian Scholarly

First published 2019 by
Australian Scholarly Publishing Pty Ltd
7 Lt Lothian St Nth, North Melbourne, Vic 3051
Tel: 03 9329 6963 / Fax: 03 9329 5452
enquiry@scholarly.info / www.scholarly.info

ISBN 978-1-925801-96-5

Cover: The suburban night sky over Southern California. Twinsday at English Wikipedia. Creative Commons Attribution-Share Alike 3.0 Unported license

Cover design: Wayne Saunders

This is the peace that comes
from being more than one.

For my parents
John and Caroline

Contents

Preface viii

Part One

1. Dear Redgate 3
2. Historical Poetics 7
3. Heavy Journalism 11
4. Notes of a Gumbarli 21
5. Big Box Island 28
6. The Next Suburb Over 37

Interlude

Suburbanist 6014 51

Part Two

7. The Poet in Suburbia 63
8. Birds of a Mirror 68
9. Notes of a Malayali 73
10. Theory Ordinaire 86
11. Archipelago Republic 99
12. From Redgate 104

Conclusion 110

Appendix: Keywords for Suburbanists 113

Acknowledgements 118

Preface

This book was written in many lands – Lenape, Wurundjeri, Whadjuk, Malayali, Wardandi, Ngarluma. I give thanks to the country, the spirits and the people, past, present and future. Without all of them, this would not have been possible. Readers are warned that this book contains words from deceased people.

The snow is thick on the ground and it is well past midnight. My housemates are asleep, but I am working. Every now and then, I hear drunken voices on the street below or a car drive past with music pumping out or a short burst of gunshot followed by sirens. It does not interrupt me. I have grown used to the sounds of the city late at night. I have been that voice and in that car. My house, this house, has been shot before.

I work through it all. A book by Hegel is spread in front of me with more notes than blank space. Wittgenstein and Weber are keeping watch nearby, and, there are stacks of new history books and old poetry ones. I am reading and writing my way through grad school here in Philadelphia. My desk is an old door on two milk crates and I have no chair. My bed is a mattress on the floor. On my walls there is an upside down map of the world and a family photograph. I am alone and I am learning and I tell myself that I am happy.

The next day, like all the other days, I walk past burned down houses and abandoned lots, past dime stores and empty restaurants, past potholes and faded murals. This neighborhood thrives in other seasons, when the light is brighter and people sit on stoops, hanging out, talking loud; but winter mutes us all.

It changes as I get closer to the university. The sky does not seem as grey as it did just ten blocks before and I can hear people talking about their research and their a-cappella group and their holidays in Vermont. The buildings sparkle, the snow is piled neatly, and security guards smile at you if it looks like you belong. I can walk without fear of falling. I can run if I want to, maybe even fly a little.

In our seminars, my classmates and I talk about the history of children or globalisation's effect on literature or how to abolish the prison system. At other times, I go to the mahogany and leather room on the top floor of the library and read through Shakespeare's *First Folio* or an illuminated manuscript or the *Codex Serafini*. It is a privileged life on the inside of one of the world's best universities. I have a sense though, that all is not right, not for me, not for the world outside. And, without rhyme or reason, without too much thought at all, in the middle of winter, I decide I cannot go on. I cannot be the historian they are making me into. I must go home.

Home is where the sun is shining and the sky is blue, where the murders are front-page news, where equality is spoken of in earnest tones, where my family belongs, where the snow never falls. All I want is to be there, floating in the ocean until the darkness comes to swallow me whole. It will take me years to realise that home is not a place at all, but a practice and a hope and a possibility that always grows. Home for me was not to be found in history, not to be found in grad school, not to be found in winter. Home is a poetic idea that is in my hands alone. Home is something to work for. Home means being safe on the waves of life itself as we suffer and toil and come to rest on islands that dreamt of us long before.

*

I am doing well at the University of Pennsylvania when I decide to leave. I love reading for hours on end and my grades are excellent; my supervisors are attentive and intelligent and push me more than I could have expected; I have co-founded an anti-war activist group and we have had some recent successes with weapons divestment; I have a large network of friends who are supportive and generous; my students respect me as a teacher and are dynamic in our classes together; I am involved in local sport and community arts; I host a weekly potluck with people from my food co-op; and I even have a mentor who teaches me about my self in ways that I cannot imagine. Despite all this, something gnaws at me. Life is full yet it does not overflow. It does not brim let alone burst. It is not enough.

I have a desire to live poetically. I long for justice, pleasure, and beauty to be threaded through my daily existence. I want the snow to fall and the sun to shine *at the same time*. I want to exalt in the paradoxes of life and to shout it from the rooftops so that others know what I care for. I want to live in the world rather than a cave of my own making let alone one of theirs. I want to be a good person.

It is four months between my decision to leave and the day I fly out of the country. In that time, I dutifully complete my masters, maintain my friendships, and teach my classes. In every spare waking hour, I turn abandoned lots into community gardens. If I felt that being a historian was not what I want to do, the gardens are what keep me going. Cleaning, planting, paving, cultivating, tending become a routine that ground me. In this way, I am doing something about global warming and becoming closer to my local community. It is this practice where I see that Hegel, Weber and Wittgenstein are not my only truth, no matter how much I love them and will continue to. Together, however, they help me find a way forward, give me a language, provide me with tools to make meaning from the soil alone. I find words in them that I hold onto while the world is burning – in 'dissemblance' I see what comes after 'deconstruction', in 'family resemblance' how we might overcome 'othering', in 'ideal types' a way around 'disciplines'. And that might matter if we walk down the path of philosophy, but I care more about the earth now, and the worms do not mind what I call them, as long as the birds stay away and leave them in the dirt to play.

My home, my truth, my *tarruru* is to be found in trees and people and poetry; in hopes and dreams and stars we cannot see; in the books that have not yet been written and the words that we birth from our imagined communities. And, as much as everyone has come here, to America, it is not where I am from. I have to go on. I have to go home, and, once I find the truth, I will have more work to do. I will have to prepare the ground for those who are forgotten or refused or neglected, those who are homeless and want to belong. That is what it is to be a poet speaking about life itself. That is a role I will come to embrace as much as learning and gardening and being a community member in a winter that feels like it will go on forever. This is about caring for the orchards and the forests and the mountains of thought, about teaching the people who have come to listen to the birds in the concrete jungle at subway stations and parking lots, about finding truth and home and peace in the world beyond its valleys, beyond these shores. It is about finding oneself as a poet for other people and the places they belong to; about stopping, for a moment, to pause in ports to offer peace where there is conflict and strife and anger throughout.

In the years after, I will go to dinner parties, sports events and gallery openings, and when I am there I will I tell people that I am that poet. I say this as a fact of life, not with shame or pride or indifference. It is what it is, and, it is where I have come to rest. Some will confess 'I used to write poetry'. Others are brave enough to declare 'I don't really like poetry'. Or, they will simply say 'My uncle is a poet'. Those are all common responses in my experience. Yet, I do not want to understand why people stop writing poetry, why others do not like poetry, or to ask who their uncles are. I simply want to celebrate the poetry that matters to me, to explain why I feel at home inside it, and to tell the story of where it has taken me since that winter. And so, this is a story of why poetry matters; how it has helped me in my own life; why it is valuable in our communities; how we can encourage each other to read, write and perform poetry; and what finding the right poetry might mean for you. It is not that poetry makes nothing happen. It is that it might make *everything* happen. It does this in communities that are truly local even as they stretch the world over.

The people I have spoken with have been humble, open, supportive, fair, and respectful throughout. We have had a lot of fun together, and so, *Suburbanism* is an act of homage to those ordinary subjects who have let me into their lives. Together, we continue to embrace what we all share – a love of language in its truest expressions. Together, we are gardeners and foragers and custodians in the wild and lush and expansive land of words, just as we exalt and praise and shout from the highest rooftops of the buildings that scrape the clouds, just as we come to reflect on ourselves in our home suburbs. The world belongs to its poets and we are happy to share it with everyone else. With other poets who came here before, and those who will come after, we are there to make you herald the dawn no matter where you come from or where you stand or if you would rather the ocean swallowed you whole and you never got tomorrow, never saw *marduggalyi*, that moment after dawn.

*

Suburbanism is a book about that moment when the sun rises. It is about the world, about identity, and matter and space and spirit and being and life itself. It is about all that the suburbs can be and uses the language that we have currently. It comes from a combination of common sense theory, dialectical critique, and sociological observation. It comes, in some way, from a conversation between Hegel and Wittgenstein and Weber as our contemporaries. It is a poetics that is philosophically informed and responsive to the daily; half tractatus, half weather report; all suburbanist, all the time.

Suburbanism is about how our place, people, and relationships can be renewed by thinking poetically. It is about how we can live in our suburbs with a utopian spirit in order to make our world better materially. After all, being true to the suburbs means retrofitting illumination with the lightning strike of the earnest larrikin. In this, there have been several texts that have mattered to me, several references that express my own reading, writing, thinking, listening, and watching. Different readers will see different affinities, but I quote others only in order to better express myself. It is with these others that we can begin to articulate who we are as individuals. They are our good neighbours in a coalition of solidarity that sees the suburbs for their beauty, reflected and refracted and mirrored truly.

I believe in a poetics that can lead to enlightenment, *bodhi, tarruru*. That insight is just as important as the work of carpenters, farmers, nurses, cooks, public servants, lawmen, all of who are as valued as the royals, the presidents, the bosses, and the Gods above and below. This not only situates the poet as a truth teller, as a person to speak back to power, but as someone who has returned from the depths, from death, from the circle, the cave, the beyond, who can speak with humble authority on what it is to belong, about why we are here, about how we can live together, unfolding with grace, dignity, fortune, generosity, and grace. This is someone with consciousness.

My consciousness, at least for this book, is about an identity from the suburbs. This identity is the suburbanist, an identity one learns and becomes, and if that comes somewhat slowly, then we must value what it is to listen despite our difficulty, to hear the whispers of the body, spirit, mind, to know what it is to go against desire and what it is to embrace duty, obligation, responsibility. For in the dawn hour, when the birds and crickets and frogs wake and stir, they can hear their calling, which asks them to voice what matters most to life itself. The country lives with them as do the ancestors and the community. They must listen to that before they begin to write and speak, before they can join a conversation with the classics, with tradition, with a worldly literature.

They can work in any language we know of, but it matters whom we are speaking to and what for. And so, for all those who want to live truly in the suburbs, know that you matter, know that your places can be as good as your words. You must also know that in our suburbs every single heart can break every single second of every single day but in that breaking it can help our futures. It can help us be remade. That is worth getting up for in the morning, working all day, and dancing the night away. *Suburbanism* will encourage you in this task no matter if your postcode is unknown, no matter if every minute is long and the light never comes, and no matter if you do not know the song. That is what it is to speak with a heart of gold pulsing with hope. That is the truth of suburbanism in this new world here and now.

*

If I once sat reading by myself with sirens in the background, now I often spend my time talking with others about today's world from its challenges to its possibilities to its questions. Since that lonely winter, I have come to be a student of the muses, to kneel at the foot of the masters, and to find home in the hearts of others. This is what it is to be a poet after history. This is what it is to return to what I already knew when it was well past midnight and the snow covered the ground all those years ago. This is what it is to be a poet who is always for the world, who swims in joy itself.

PART ONE

1

Dear Redgate

We are in New York, as far away as we can be, the other side of the world from you. It took a day to get here, a day sitting in a tin can that we will never get back. But, New York makes the journey seem worthwhile. It is, after all, the capital of the world and it makes me reflect on where I have come from, how I came to be here, and what I have done. It makes me think of you. I wonder what you are, dear Redgate. Are you a hamlet? A village? A suburb? What do you make of the Indian Ocean that borders you on that western coast? Of the towns you are close to? What of the country that you are in? Are you a place for suburbanists? Of suburbanism? What comes next for you, Redgate? Those questions press on me here.

We are living on the Upper West Side, or to be more precise, on 84th Street between Riverside Drive and West End Avenue, a couple of blocks west of Broadway. Down the end of the street you can see the Hudson River. Our building is an old brownstone that has been carved into apartments, and, on the stairs, there is worn and torn red carpet where one can see the dirt from glory days that are long gone. We have plenty of natural light and a stove that works, which are all one really needs. It doesn't matter that we are not in Bushwick or that we will have mice, a gas leak, frozen pipes.

It is autumn here, and, in the morning, I walk to work at Columbia University. I vary my route each day. Some days I walk up Broadway, others up Amsterdam, still others yet by the river. No matter which way I go, I walk past more people than I have ever seen on your beaches, more people than all those who have watched us surfing, swimming or diving. The people here are so different from one to another. It seems the whole world is here in this little stretch of concrete and glass, asphalt and grass. They walk past me as I walk past them, and no one says 'hello' even as we momentarily glance at each other. It is never a gaze, never enough time to lock eyes, not to stare. I don't stop to chat, and, in that way, it is so unlike you, dear Redgate, where strangers pause and comment.

At the university, I sit in Butler Library and read all day. I only break for lunch. I went once to the Hungarian Pastry Shop and once to Shake Shack, but neither of them was my kind of place. The first is too far from my desk, and, the second is just fast food. Instead, I go to the Hamilton Deli and get a turkey wrap. I have never eaten much turkey at home, but here it is so common, like squash or yam or corn. In the late afternoons, I meet up with K. We talk about our days as we walk in a different neighbourhood, stare through windows at things we cannot yet afford, get blisters on blisters on our feet.

Sometimes we go to bookstores and browse, think about what our library will look like when we have our own home. The other night we went to Book Culture and I bought the October issue of *Poetry* for $3.75. It was the first time I had opened its covers and there was one poem I liked. I read it right there on Columbus Ave:

In the Kitchen
by Chen Jun

Early in the morning a dough rises from the bowl
curling upward.
He clenches his fists of bean paste, his mouth
dripping a black cocoa stream …
Hey, I say, have you just smuggled
nine knife mountains and nine oil pans from hell?
Deep-fried ghosts are the sweetest the crispiest the most intelligent
even in burned rims, and taste even better with soybean drinks.
He droops his sad expressions
like Oedipus's crutch.

Collapsed in the steamer, he squeaks out a sweet smell
of duck soup from his soul – quack, quack.
Translated from the Chinese by Ming Di

I like 'deep-fried ghosts' and 'quack quack', and I laugh a little at the poem, stand still while the traffic swirls and the people with dogs stoop to pick up shit. We walk home up Broadway, watching people with bread under their arms and baseball caps on.

It is interesting to think of America, or to be more precise New York, or to be more precise, this place right here and now, as being in the centre. It is an old idea that all centres are made by their peripheries; that the people who come to make it here think that they can make it anywhere. Yet, this 'here' is nowhere to be found and one must simply take pleasure in one's surrounds. You must embrace the stage before the audience is made or the play has been settled on. You cannot go anywhere because you have already been found.

We like it in our neighbourhood. Some days, we sit and read in Central Park, and in *World Literature Today*, there was an interview with an Argentinian labourer called Kike. He says:

> The importance of literature is that I write the best I can and that my tools are good, to *work* the story, to *work* the words, to *work* the language. And later, what those words are going to say is what you have. If you are a person who watches TV shows and likes karate that is going to translate into your *work*. In my case, I write for my union's magazine, and like you say, I am a political activist. I am a person with deep political convictions, which I express everywhere. So that too is in my literature. But it is obvious that it is going to be there because that is part of who I am. And everything that I am comes out in my literature whether I want it to be there or not.

All of it is there in the writing all the time, even now, even here where

New York and its ghosts and its dough and its workers shadow this very page. Here, you can see the steps you made on the walk that was as long as the island, as tall as the skyscrapers, as wide as the dreams that turned to dust under the million stars that you can never see here, not from our place on the third floor of a brownstone you walk up after a day reading elsewhere.

Just as I cannot see the stars, I cannot see the limits of my self, and here, particularly, one realises the possibilities of what one is not, of how the questions and the answers are so specific, so determined by the frame of reference that is not yours alone to find the boundary of. And so, one begins to think through 'New York' even as one needs to think through one's body in the language of one's own making – my self in a city, my self in America, my self in a world that can be intelligible beyond the logic of my kidneys, lungs, feet, knees, capillaries. This world contains bodies within it; multitudes that we can see and sing of, that we can glimpse despite the shadows, that we can begin to outline in our letters and our words and our sentences in the hope that we change it a little, that we give a hot meal to you and them and our selves instead of cold soup made only from stones and buttons and broken dreams and nettles and thorns. Maybe we all need to do is to break bagels together. Maybe you should come over to our brownstone and speak about this place in the world.

I think of this as you, dear Redgate, are warming my marrow from inside. I carry you in me and you help me go on. Sometimes, I think of what it would be like to bring a little New York to you, a little Upper West Side, and Columbia to your beaches and your people. Could that be a food cart for when we come out of the surf? Could that be a plaque like the one for Rachmaninoff at the end of my block? Could that be a library that has the names of Virgil, Socrates, Homer on it? I do not know the answer to those questions and I do not care. I love you the way you are. At this time of year, I love the spider orchids and how they tangle at the base of the jarrah. I love the cool of the water and how it makes my hairs stand on end. I love the way the light comes through the leaves and is soft with golden wheatiness. I love you to the moon and back, in my body and the world, through and through. I will see you soon, dear Redgate, soon.

2

Historical Poetics

As a child growing up in the suburbs, I was not exposed to a wide range of poetry. My father, conscious of his Scottish roots, had a volume of my namesake, Robbie Burns, by his bedside from which he regularly quoted and my Indian mother used nursery rhymes, proverbs, and limericks as moral lessons for my sisters and I, mentioning the subcontinent's own Rabi (Tagore) as someone I myself should read. But 'poetry' itself was not held apart, or considered to be of greater importance than times tables, capital city memorisation, dinosaur identification, finger painting, or even family knowledge.

When I went to university I read history – my father had written a dissertation on British economists and the empire in the 19th century and my mother had studied the connection between Impressionism and psychology. My own turn to the past seemed like an inheritance. I soon discovered that if one searches for the start of a fire one may find it everywhere and not only in lightning. This holds for a historian of the Annales School or of a structuralist persuasion or simply the common sense practical critic, each of whom choose a 'point x' from where they can definitively declare that this is the beginning of a history that follows.

History is concerned with time, and in so far as one wants to declare it being about 'change over time' one might also draw attention to similarity over time, tied as those two are in a dialectical embrace. What the historian concerns themselves with is not simply the facts, that which happened, but an unrecognised ground, ladder, and sky that might be best thought of as the games of politics, philosophy, and poetry, which are the genres my type of history borrowed from. In interrogating what the underlying principles are, one must bring to the surface what we commonly hold to be depth. What seems superficial or self-indulgent or artificial assumes an importance precisely because of its particularity, of how it can be hidden beneath.

That we can focus on the look of the body as a history, assumed in politics to be a distinct and inalienable source of private property, means that birth, literally and metaphorically, is used as a beginning. This might be for convenience or congealment, simply because 'it makes sense' or that's 'just what you do'. The other paradigmatic introduction is often the metonymic one – the single acorn anecdote that contains within it the whole of the oak forest discourse. There is also the history that places two events side-by-side as if comparing oak to karri. These may be the established ways of writing history, but they are not the only ones. What holds for them is a type of prose that values linearity and clarity, a type of progress, and a certain peer review.

After I studied history, I studied poetry in a metropolitan centre of contemporary experimentalism. Poetics in this iteration is often attuned to how the story is told, to the *form* of the essay, and in so doing it may mimic, and hence mock, the journalistic article, or continue the practice of abstraction, claiming to radically break down prose itself. That one may get lost in this thicket of irony and difficulty suggests that the centre of this world displays an exhaustive, contemporary archival network, and, that the expectations of what constitutes radical, avant-garde, or peripheral relies on an expectation of what is conservative, dominant, or normal. In this poetics, the historical sediment of what once was official is not broken down into its component parts but held aloft as a straw man made for beating.

The question after that might be, what does world historical poetry look like to me? If we broke this into its constitutive parts we might be tempted to say the world is too big to comprehend, that history is about time and being, and poetry is a self-expression. And that might be the case, for all of these positions can be defended in the language games of conferences and academic papers. World historical poetry implies that it is a particular literary expression of world historical spirit, of the collective reason of a country whose custodians make it poetic. The inevitability of one's own perspective, the limited frame of reference, the realisation that the 'nation' matters, means that in searching for what comes to be 'spirit' is bound with language as a thought process. But, what some call spirit we might call death. If we can leave taxes to the Marxists, thinking through death means examining the life lived. The point might not be to explain it, through experience or reference or knowledge, but simply to take stock of how you spent your time in the places you visited with the people you knew best. And so, we come back to history if not to poetics.

History sees and poetics interprets. History is that which observes the face and represses its desire to say it is beautiful or ugly, even as it must, whereas poetics does the opposite. History works by accumulation, poetics by interrogation. History goes with contextual aggregation through the reading of several texts. Poetics uses close inspection through the reading of one text. Or so it appears in the disciplinary regime of today's university. Says the historian 'if the poet has no eye for the world, we cannot understand them', which might account for the lack of a sociological poetics. The paradox, however, is that history may do the work of close reading through its apparent lack of interpretation just as poetics carries with it a whole host of contextual judgement, which we can take account of simply by reading symptomatically. Historical poetics is the fact that 'one man might make an accurate drawing of the two faces, and the other notices in the drawing the likeness which the former did not see.'

We cannot help but live with sociological categories, which are abstractions grounded in material histories, just as we cannot live without philosophical assumptions (seen in the use of specific words such as 'dialectics'), political 'realities' (how knowledge is disseminated) and linguistic metaphors (see Hegel on the fire). Each word is a madeleine and a child of midnight. The move away from nationalism's collective madeleines be they parrots or kangaroos or Southern Cross tattoos fails to think through the way there is a universalising language whose root is closer to me as a lived material reality than if I was in London. Within walking distance of here I can find a kangaroo that is not in a zoo, in a book or on a screen. This is a return of the repressed real when all appears digital, when our moment in history seems conditional. What are the words of a world language that we have here because there is always a world and always a here?

Should we then 'mistrust our own senses but not our own beliefs' or should we acknowledge that 'the human body is the best picture of the human soul'? I have been subject to attempts to categorise me as poet in a particular way, many as shorthand for my embodiment – as straight, as bourgeois, as minority, as person of colour, as male. Rather than refuse such designations as boundaries of confinement, I would prefer to interrogate the assumptions that underpin their common ground while maintaining useful and affective bonds with individual actors themselves. In other words, what is the logic behind the identification and how can we ask that *with* someone, and hence begin work on a collaborative project that is utopian in its premise rather than simply inherited. This extends to each word and is based on the acknowledgement that a new criterion for seeing and interpretation 'can conceal the old problem but not solve it.' That is one such task for the poetics that has me in its sights.

In 'Lectures on the Philosophy of World History', Hegel puts paid to any notion that history teaches us lessons now precisely because of the particularities of each situation, which is not to say that universal spirit, divine reason or the world itself are absent, but that historians may not be well equipped to translate their teaching to the present. He is not wholly wrong even as he is not wholly right. One task for the contemporary poet is to continue to find hope in the languages of our present not as transcendence of history, or politics or bodies or spirits or country, but as a way of thinking through a collective past that is the material ground upon which to build a house in the suburb of language itself. And while the future may be hidden from us, it does not stop the astronomer from calculating the eclipse of the sun or me from wearing shades when I go to the beach on Christmas Day when I am home for the summer.

3

Heavy Journalism

Poetics becomes a space into which one can write of oneself and the world. Its parents are ideas and life in the broadest sense of those terms. For ideas, I think philosophically. For life, I read the newspaper. This is where we come to 'heavy journalism'. It is comfortable with the classics of thought be they East or West, North or South, but it is also a type of vernacular that reminds one of a pizza order. It could also be called 'theory ordinaire'. The negation of heavy journalism is to be found in the unsuccessful combination of the same elements, which are not synthesised dialectically, a kind of suburbanite fake news and a stolid peer review.

To write heavy journalism, we could think of Boccaccio when he writes:

> You must read, you must persevere, you must sit up nights, you must inquire, and exert the utmost power of your mind. If one way does not lead to the desired meaning, take another; if obstacles arise, then still another; until, if your strength holds out, you will find that clear which at first looked dark.

And so, heavy journalism is the style in which to share clarity. When it is written:

> … it can arm kings, marshal them for war, launch whole fleets from their docks, nay, counterfeit sky, land, sea, adorn young maidens with flowery garlands, portray human

> character in its various phases, awake the idle, stimulate the dull, restrain the rash, subdue the criminal, and distinguish excellent people with their proper meed of praise.

In distinguishing excellent people, heavy journalism reflects on what it is to be together, to find in the combination of rigor and delight a type of insight that allows you to come closer to *tarruru* than was ever possible before.

*

Heavy journalism lies somewhere between, like the suburbs themselves. They are between the city and the country, a liminal space that feels good to rest in, a type of twilight. As Plato says:

> In fact, anyone with any sense would remember that the eyes can become confused in two different ways, as a result of two different sets of circumstances: it can happen in the transition from light to darkness, and also in the transition from darkness to light.

Between darkness and light, between philosophy and journalism, between theory and the ordinary, we only know what one is when we can see the other. Light is only light because we can *see* the dark. It is all transitions then, always confusing, all on a spectrum of sight and blindness that language helps us make sense of. It is 'light' and 'dark' after all. But who is there to name it so?

That is for the poet. You may know them by other names – philosopher, historian, teacher – but the poet is the worker in language, the one who names the world. And that is a brave and foolish endeavour. As Aristotle says, 'the art of poetry belongs to the genius or the mad person.' It is only the genius or the mad person who would name the world rather than live according to their stomach. It is up to the suburbanites, the community, the readers to decide if the mad person is a genius, if the genius is a mad person. Those suburbanites are the ones who name the poet even as the poet names their world. But, how does a poet know what to name themself?

That comes from other people. That comes from the ground that has been struck by lightning. That comes from planting seeds in the decomposing bodies of ancestors. The poet can sense what is their island and what is their death consciousness. If they do not know who they are, and if neither do we, then we must look to their material, to their world. In Horace's words, 'you poets must choose material equal to your powers.' And so, with that knowledge of what our life truly is, we rename the suburbs of our selves, be that from historian to poet, from worker to dreamer, from teacher to seer. We are, after all, in suburbs of language, making our lives through the words we know in a sea that is as infinite and limitless as all the possibilities beyond the reach of the dying. It is the heavy journalist who carries the reports of the poets who come back from the other side.

*

But, if we know what heavy journalism is, what then is the 'colonised' poet to do? How are they to escape the colonial situation and move themselves and their people towards a true liberation? The answers to those questions depend partly on what the empire is, and so, we must ask who is responsible for the chains that I am in?

The empire that has us shackled is death. Even as one cannot fear what comes next, death is a logical end point that we must work against and not only with a simple celebration of life itself. We can decolonise into life as a whole. I could detail the ways in which I am oppressed, claim loudly that I am a man of colour, say how my grandparents were not born free in colonial India, speak of how I myself am not yet in a republic, but that would only be half a story that does not detail how truly privileged I am, by lifestyle, imagination, and habitus.

But this is not a story about me. This is a story about the nation of suburbs in which I live, a story about the mirror stage of the colony, and what it might mean when we think about mimesis and becoming. As Frantz Fanon has said, 'the poverty of the people, national oppression, and the inhibition of culture are one and the same thing.' This is a lesson about unlearning inhibition as much as it is about the paradoxes that I see here. Seeing paradox is, of course, one of the conditions of liberty from death. We must come to realise that contradictions are essential for living. And so, we should not reify the end but merely look beyond it by looking before it.

We could say of death, what Fanon said of the nation:

> … far from keeping aloof from other nations, therefore, it is national liberation which leads the nation to play its part on the stage of history. It is at the heart of national consciousness that international consciousness lives and grows. And this two-fold emerging is ultimately only the source of all culture.

This means that we must come to discuss the death of our life and the life of our death. And that means, in our case, coming into an understanding of the end of our colonial inheritance. In the field of poetry, that means letting go of the belief that English alone is relevant for representing life here, means letting go of the kneeling before Anglophone masters from a canon of the long dead. In means forging our own path, reconciled to its place as a responsible global citizen. We cannot imitate what we think we should be doing. Instead, we must find our own direction. As Hegel said 'by mere imitation art cannot stand in competition with nature, and, if it tries, it looks like a worm trying to crawl after an elephant.' We are too often worms while History, New York, death are elephants.

We have to go our own way, structurally and symptomatically, but we might yet believe that we can find new ways to fight, together. What we must look at then, as heavy journalists writing about poets, is what Edward Said asked us to look at:

> … style, figures of speech, setting, narrative devices, historical and social circumstance, *not* the correctness of the representation nor its fidelity to some great original.

Such attentiveness will mean that we do not obsess over origin points nor where we come from in some grand sense. What lies before us is something to work with. It is something worth writing about in such a way that we might develop an understanding of our selves, where we come from and what we might yet become. All reality, like all life, must sit next to all representation, all death. That is where the direction of the paradox emerges and becomes dialectical. So, what is 'death' and how does that matter for authority? Can we say that Ralph Emerson or TS Eliot have died? Or do they still live because their words are with us? What is it to die if one pays attention to the body of work and not just the body that wrote the words? And how might this mean something for the poetry we compose as we decompose even if we are still here?

Eliot writes that:

> No poet, no artist of any art, has their complete meaning alone. Their significance, their appreciation is the appreciation of their relation to the dead poets and artists. You cannot value them alone; you must set them, for contrast and comparison, among the dead.

The dead here would seem to be self-explanatory, but it is another thing to recover the minor poets who are living that are forgotten by 'the world'. It is yet another to suggest that one can be measured against the names that linger longer.

Some would have us believe that there is an inverse relationship in this; that the more one knows about the past, the more influential one will be; the more one can stand above it all and survey the land before us. A giant on the shoulders of short ones stacked tall. But, this is to assume and hope in facts alone. There needs to be a guiding principle, which is to say that we need a philosophy of the dead to go with our naming of the individual. This is there when Eliot suggests:

> What is to be insisted upon is that the poet must develop or procure the *consciousness* of the past and that they should continue to develop this consciousness throughout their career.

What is consciousness, but a philosophical reality that you live with as you go on through life itself? But, did you notice the slippage I allowed when I let Eliot substitute 'past' for 'dead'? What then is a death consciousness as opposed to a simple past one? That might be where we have *Geist*, which is to say a type of spirit, as opposed to simple historical apprehension. This is because death, if it is anything, is a trick that gets us to think that a chapter was closed or that a person has gone or that an era has ended even as we apprehend them in new ways that suggest the very opposite. They persist, they live on, they are not gone. Death consciousness is not the same as historical consciousness, just like heavy journalism is not popular theory.

But, death is the great leveler; something we can all reckon with, a thing that is democratic even if it is as distinct as the lives we live. The life of the poet must somehow understand the life of Others, including those who are dead and those who are unseen by death. They must climb inside that mind, not to know the facts of life but their spirit, what lives after them. In Emerson's thinking, they are:

> … the student of the world; and of what the world is worth, and with what emphasis it accosts the soul of humanity, such is the worth, such is the call of the poet.

The poet is the student of the world spirit who knows:

> … the world is theirs, but they must possess it by putting themself in harmony with the constitution of things. They must be a solitary, laborious, modest and charitable soul.

The student that is the poet has their ground in the popular tradition, which is to say they must see that the opposite of death is the life of the people they represent, and through that come to an understanding of what it is to see the end, to be a journalist writing of the daily bread and a philosopher dealing with the heaviness of existence.

*

In a time of climate change, one realises that 'nature' has been poisoned, wrecked, polluted. It is harder to maintain the simply transcendent line of argument when we look around and see the Pacific Trash Vortex, the tailings of mines, the smog in Delhi, Beijing, Rio, Lagos, Mexico City. And yet there is something to the writing of a prior era that can help us think about our moment now, not only as natural beings in the world, but as people connected to structures beyond ourselves.

After all, the dead poets knew that the mines and factories in their own days imperilled nature. They could see the frontier as it was closing, could see that nature required our attention and care. It not only meant one had to work to be connected to the natural world, connected to birds and bees and parrots and orchids, but also that one had to mediate relationships between individuals and systems, between sports reports and treatises.

How do we find those systems? How do we know what we connect to? For that, we must know, as Emerson suggests that the 'human is that noble endogenous plant which grows... from within outward.' That inward-outwardness exists because 'a person is a bundle of relations, a knot of roots, whose flowers and fruitage is the world.' But, are they unique, are we unique, like snowflakes as the cliché holds or are we a knot of roots as Emerson would have us believe? He seems like the original defender of unoriginal genius, writing:

> No great poets are original. Nor does valuable originality consist in unlikeliness to other poets … The greatest genius is the most indebted poet … There is no choice to genius.

This is to say, the genius samples like a bowerbird, a magpie, a crocodile. They occupy the space between 'infinite Reason' and the 'heart and sense of the crowd', between the philosopher and the journalist, the historian and the poet, the living and the dead. To do this, they need nature as something that they are part of, networked to, an aspect of themselves, and which they can express from inside out. For:

> … genius detects through the fly, through the caterpillar, through the grub, through the egg, the content individual… through all the kingdoms of organised life the eternal unity. Nature is a mutable cloud, which is always and never the same.

It is on us then to know that we can 'deal with worlds and pebbles freely.' And so we can see that next to the yam is the pebble and next to the pebble is a world that was made over and over and over again by the people who are tilling the soil; those who know that nature is a cloud and an egg and a corpse as well.

*

Philosophy and journalism are bedfellows or cousins or twins or siblings or rivals or all of the above depending on whom you ask. They bear a family resemblance, but what is their ancestral root and what is their branch of difference and distinction? I do not ask this to ask whether the charismatic authority of any one individual can do both together. Rather, what are the qualities that make philosophy philosophy and journalism journalism as they have been understood already? I hesitate here too, though more precisely because I am a writer interested in poetics that is a bridge between these two worlds. And so, I think of John Keats when he states:

> A poet is the most unpoetical of anything in existence, because they have no Identity – they are continually in,

> for and filling some other body. The Sun – the Moon – the Sea, and men and women and people, who are creatures of impulse, are poetical, and have about them an unchangeable attribute; the poet has none, no identity – they are certainly the most unpoetical of all God's creatures.

Could we then say that the most unphilosophical of all the world's creatures is the philosopher? The most unjournalistic is the journalist? Is the heavy journalist as light as hot air? To answer that is not quite so simple, precisely because Keats did not make it simple.

Even if this 'negative capability' means 'a person is capable of being in uncertainties, mysteries, doubts, without any irritable reaching after fact and reason', it does not follow that this should determine their being as if it were a master key of identity that rendered a poet capable of rejecting the thesis itself. And the same would apply for the philosopher and the journalist too even if reason and fact were what determined them as well. This is precisely because it is a pure negation rather than an antithetical negotiation. And, at the end of the day, Keats died too, and, in so doing he came to a resolution, which was one end in this world. It does not take a philosopher or a journalist to see that, though there is something heavy and contemporary about saying it so. His words live, however, they are here as well, even if no-one has words that are his to claim, not even how we link them.

And, besides, what of how philosophy and journalism have changed since Keats wrote? And, have they changed no thanks to philosophers and journalists but because of the mechanics and labourers of History instead? A history not of the individual, but the context around them be that machines and ecologies, legislation and companies, dogs and swine?

This might be what could lead Jean Baudrillard to argue that, 'if it no longer aspires to a discourse of truth, philosophy must assume the form of a world from which truth has withdrawn.' Philosophy has taken the place of fact and reason, Truth with a capital T, common sense common to commoners like the newspapers that no longer circulate in our digital age.

What is the grey space, what is the liminal centre, what is that space where truth is neither present nor absent? To ask this is to agree with Baudrillard that:

> If the world is hardly compatible with the concept of the real we impose upon it, the function of philosophy is certainly not to reconcile, but on the contrary, to seduce, to wrest things from their condition, to force them into an over-existence which is incompatible with the real. Even if it speaks of surpassing the economic, philosophy itself cannot be an economy of discourse. To speak about excess and sacrifice, it must become excessive and sacrificial.

It is to say, the old antagonism between philosophy and journalism, between poetry and poetics, between the long-winded reflection and the sound-bite update, seems precisely that – old. We must not, of course, assume that the old is redundant, useless, in need of renovation. Rather, one must apprehend its qualities and ask what should I read in light of the novel? Is it Aristotle or Sappho, when the world is ablaze with Herodotus and the cable channel? Or maybe, just maybe, those Greeks alone are not enough and it is time to turn to the conversations around us that make the debate between philosophy and journalism seem important once more? That might be the next task of a heavy journalist looking at their suburbs right now.

4

Notes of a Gumbarli

It is important to note that I have been visiting the Pilbara for fifteen years, and, have made trips there in 2003, 2006, 2008, 2011, 2014, and 2018, and always with permission from traditional owners. After all, I recognise the Ngardas of that ngurra and the continuing contribution they make as experts in keeping the world safe, diverse, dynamic, open, and welcoming. The material for this essay on tjabi was gathered during archival work since 2011 and as part of two projects on country in 2014 and 2018, which took me to Port Headland, Yandeyarra, Roebourne, Karratha, Croydon Station, and Millstream. These were organised by Tarruru, a Ngarluma owned organisation. I want to thank my gumbarli (brother-in-law/sister's husband) Andrew Dowding for asking me to help him out, and, for introducing me to a number of community members and kin. You can find out more about tjabi through Andrew's own work, including his forthcoming dissertation 'Yirrama Computer: locating Pilbara tjabi traditions in the modern world', which was written at the Wilin Centre from the University of Melbourne. His views take precedence and should be regarded as authoritative. I simply want to share my perspective on what we have learnt together. I also want to celebrate the Elders we collaborated with, which allowed me to hear people sing in language, to watch the repatriation of an institutionalised archive, and to spend time in homes, in public space, and on country. At the end of the day, there is nothing quite like hearing tjabi where it comes from and seeing people enjoy being together. Thanks go to song poets Frank Brown, Kerry Churnside, Charlie Coppin, Peter Jeffries, Alice Mitchell, Biddy Norman, Irene Roberts, Stephen Stewart, David Stock, Bruce Thomas,

Alec Tucker and David Walker. Thanks also go to Jill Churnside for having us over for dinner as Sufi poets sang in the background. It was an honour and privilege to spend time with everyone, and, I am looking forward to next time. If readers are interested in performance of tjabi today, I suggest you find out more about Patrick Churnside, who is the leading contemporary song poet of his time and place.

Theodor Adorno writes that 'art exists in the real world and has a function in it, and the two are connected by a large number of links.' Those links however, the things that connect each to the other, are harder to name. What does the daily life of a protest poet look like compared to a conservative one when both work in a modern university? What poetry does the politician read? How is suburbanist poetry connected to the ideological unconscious of the country, social relations, and history it comes from?

In thinking through the activities of poets who consider themselves political, and in responding to an oversight of the literary academic record, we might want to consider poetry that is outside the official record. To that end, we need to consider the *Volk*, to think through bush ballads, spoken word, and performance poetry as political verse cultures with their own aesthetics, logic, and economy. Indeed, for all the debates within the academy there is a tacit conflict with those outside it through the absence of criticism.

This includes many Western Pilbara traditions that are often framed as ethnographic. These may be dismissed as an object of study because they are 'difficult', but we could simply update debates concerning the avant-garde to justify their inclusion in the university literary field. This means bringing poetry that escapes scrutiny into the critical realm as much as it means changing the poetics discourse around accepted texts. As A.D. Hope writes in 'The Activists' in 1965:

> In a sense, all great literature makes itself known as such by the overwhelming conviction of truth that it produces: either that enlargement of experience which astonishes us with a

> quite new vision, or that refashioning of experience which Shelley calls the power to strip 'the veil of familiarity from the world and lay bare the naked and sleeping beauty'.

Enlargement and refashioning need happen in our criticism too. We need a new vision of the fire that the larrikin started some time ago. This means we must think of *tjabi*, which is the story of sharing, of collaboration, not the 'dying race' or 'resistance' or 'survival'. We see this when we recognise the frame of *Ngardas*, and, in this piece it must be realised that people do engage with colonialism, capitalism, and the nation state, but they are not defined by it. This is about a community art form that joyfully celebrates life in its place.

Tjabi are public, open song poems of the Western Pilbara, which is a place with suburbs including quarter acre houses with backyard swimming pools to a Wendy's in the Headland mall where Elders gather today. *Tjabi* are composed from dream, and, were explained to me as independent label pop songs of their time, those 'Slim Dusty kind of ones'. Although they are regionally specific, *tjabi* are similar to other forms in other regions. Other geographies with other ideologies and worldviews have their own types of poetry, such as *jawi* in the Kimberley. And so, *tjabi* were known to travel outside the Western Pilbara including to the Gascoigne, Eastern Pilbara, and Desert.

I expect many readers have heard of songlines as well as the argument that any cultural engagement is appropriation. Critical work on *tjabi* is informed by those debates, but they are also distinct precisely because anyone can hear them, and, can write them if they want to. It won't make them an expert, or proficient, or even capable of composing a good *tjabi*. But, it is open, and so, it is a form that goes beyond its rooted cosmopolitanism, beyond its home in the Western Pilbara, having designs and possibilities just like haiku, pantuns, sonnets, ghazals, and villanelles. That these other forms have extended beyond Japan, Malaysia, Italy, Persia, and France, and their respective eras, would only suggest that *tjabi* can leave home and do well for itself. It is a diasporic subject that knows where it comes from and where it might go. After all these are personally authored works that circulate publicly rather than religious understandings and there are no cultural proscriptions that prohibit sharing them. This is reflected in the fact that *tjabi* are often reflections on daily life. Donald Norman, for example, has *tjabi* on wristwatches, aeroplanes, and station work, and, in his day, had a wide audience of women, children, non-locals, and others who had not been through Law. And yet, the people who were strong in this world are also the best *tjabi nyinirri* in town. That holds true for the past, and, it holds true for now.

In the published record of Anglophone poetics, *tjabi* are most well-known through Carl von Brandenstein and A.P. Thomas' 1974 book *Taruru*. *Tjabi* from that volume have been collected in the *Penguin Anthology of Australian Poetry*, quoted in Bonny Cassidy's *Final Theory*, and taught in university courses. They are, moreover, part of a well-developed anthropological tradition of song poetry that has been recorded by ethnomusicologists such as Bob Dixon, Ronald and Catherine Berndt, John Bradley, Alan Marrett, Linda Barwick, and Sally Treloyn. I came to *tjabi* through my *gumbarli*, who is an ethnomusicologist, and a sovereign traditional owner for *Ngarluma ngurra*. One of my favourite *tjabi* comes from his grandfather:

Mount Satirist Station
by Robert Churnside

Kangala karnamarna warrimarila,
jurndiri julajula
Narnukardi
marnda wangugurrula
ilinkarrima
puliri karba
From high up I am viewing the bare ground
The crevices, recession in diffusion
Towards Narnuna
The mountain in the corner of my view

Seems to be tearing to shreds
The rounded contours of its peak.

If, as Les Murray has written, 'settled country is the land of the dead', this work is alive, rooted, and active. Note the words 'viewing' and 'tearing'. It opposes the suburbanite who would be passive, the white settler who would simply occupy, and the Anglophonic hegemony that would only sing in English. Note the place name Narnuna, which oppose the colonial renaming undertaken by city planners and local council. It opposes the person who would simply float above country. Stylistically, the poem has a sort of plain speaking materialism – weather is central and expressing that in a common sense language matters. We are close to ordinary speech where we order milk from the corner shop for delivery.

This *tjabi*, and a poetics associated with it, enables the transformation of the objective social world because it transforms our mode of literary representation, which rests on expanding then re-interpreting the archive. This does so through the re-contextualisation and de-familiarisation that happens by virtue of consideration against a frame that would place public Western Pilbara traditions in ethnographic museums. This is because of the historical failure to consider this poetry within a literary aesthetic paradigm, which is still the case notwithstanding prior attempts. In that sense, considering *tjabi* speaks back to questions of style here, style being never more than an extension of context.

How should we consider this material as readers next to this place? If my conversations with people on country are indicative, there is a wealth of ordinary language criticism in Western Pilbara communities, a kind of theory of texts performed in colloquial Englishes. This is to say nothing of the conversations that happen in Ngarluma, Yindjibarndi, and Banjima, of the local language conversations that suggest a form of sovereignty we must open ourselves out to. This is about suggesting that our frames of reference, our reading tools, might not easily serve the same purpose for which they were designed, which is to say we cannot mimic an empirical theory either. As Stephen Colliss writes:

> … poetry's politics is to be found in *where* we find poetry – in the communal spaces it becomes a part of, the struggles it has some currency in.

We need poems from countries within this landmass to speak back to the idea of the nation. That means seeming Ngarluma land with a sense of depth, care, resilience, beauty, tradition, all of which is possible when we act as people interested in more than our own postcodes who listen to Elders and custodians. In addition, we need to begin reframing certain material as poetic and in so doing enrich what constitutes the political as it exists in the nation today. We might start by thinking of Western Pilbara *tjabi* as part of the language games that form our ideologies and worldview, and that returns us to the opening questions on politics and poetry in general.

As to its listeners, people may speak of close reading, or even close listening, but in thinking through the lived conditions of occupation in suburban societies we might want to re-examine some of the revolutionary potential of 'ear work' particularly in the Western Pilbara. Elders I spoke with asked me to just listen to the poems, to engage with the language itself. This listening, which connects to us as a reading, is a type of critical, receptive endeavour. If ear work is what we may call a type of labour, what are the specific ideas of its labouring? That depends on the text and the body of the listener. In other words, no two *tjabi* elicit the same response, and no two listeners respond in the same way, and one listener's response may change between any two listening sessions. Every new poem needs a new poetics every time it is encountered. It might also imply some differences in how we listen, or how we watch the listener, which connects us to the frame of suburbanism as immanent critique.

We might call this 'ritualisation', which is the de-habitusing of daily life, including our own, which is to say the bringing to conscious articulation what is congealed. This is listening, and hence literary criticism, as a type of intellectual dance precisely because it is consciously embodied. It might be the habitus of one person, but it is about de-familiarising our habits so we can re-cognise it in the language of the academy to help in an act of intellectual solidarity.

Thinking of habits means thinking of how a cup of tea when we first meet might become significant if our relationship develops into a meaningful one. In that way, a good life is aided and abetted by the intentionalising of that which is 'taken-for-granted'. And so, what separates ritual – in its sociological definition rather than its anthropological or everyday one – from habitus is intention. Through shared ritual we might share an empathetic openness that allows us to engage actively with the text, which is ultimately an interpretive and political act that involves creating community. This means there are fellow travellers to be found in ways that undo myths based on racialised thinking. Ear work asks us to listen to country and its custodians because it is attentive, open, and utopian. It implies that we need think through lived power relations in a historically attentive manner if we are to generate useful understandings.

Poetry, as the research and development wing of language, is thinking at the edge. It can help us precisely because difficult problems, problems endemic to the Western Pilbara, require intentional language. A self-aware poetry, of a particular social kind, can give us a critique that moves us towards solidarity in a digital age. Returning materials, allowing communities control over archives, learning languages in an appropriate way, listening to Elders, and spending time on country all matter for the society that is to come. To undertake this work means shifting power from anthropological and literary institutions towards a collaborative project that responds to the ongoing re-presentation of self in everyday life occasioned by the digital industrial complex – this is the self as artificially constructed, as mediated, as disembodied to a degree where performance is inseparable from the real. Realising that the Western Pilbara is globally connected not only through iron ore pathways, but also through the online access of poetic resources means we need think through the possibilities of our own ear work for now and tomorrow.

5

Big Box Island

According to Walt Whitman, 'the city' is a place with 'shows, architecture, customs, tradition'; 'pageants, tableaus, spectacles', 'houses, ships, wharves', 'processions', 'bright windows with goods in them'; 'marble' and 'iron'. On the other hand, the country is a place of fields with 'two little yellow butterflies shuffling between each other, ascending high in the air' where there are 'herds of cows'. It is 'a sunlit pasture field with cattle and horses feeding'.

In his poetry, Whitman travels through city and country alike, as well as through specific places that conform to these ideal types. But, he mentions the word 'suburbs' only once in *Leaves of Grass*, writing:

> I ascend to the foretruck,
> I take my place late at night in the crow's-nest,
> We sail the arctic sea, it is plenty light enough,
> Through the clear atmosphere I stretch around on the
> wonderful beauty,
> The enormous masses of ice pass me and I pass them, the
> scenery is plain in all
> directions,
> The white-topt mountains show in the distance, I fling out
> my fancies toward them,
> We are approaching some great battle-field in which we are
> soon to be engaged,

> We pass the colossal outposts of the encampment, we pass with still feet and caution,
> Or we are entering by the *suburbs* some vast and ruin'd city,
> The blocks and fallen architecture more than all the living cities of the globe.

After a period of exploration of the open natural world, the suburbs become the entry point to 'a vast and ruin'd city'. They are the transition between the arctic sea, the wonderful beauty, the masses of ice, the white-topt mountains to the 'blocks and fallen architecture more than all the living cities of the globe'. If we move from one cold location to a place without living bodies, a closed off ruin that has no pulse, Whitman has to name this and to notice how his very feet are still. The suburbs here are descriptively absent, a simple passageway between sublime places that truly exist. They are named but not defined – they are not sung of as a place, maybe because they were yet to be visible when Whitman was writing.

Whitman tends to be read as both a symptom of a popular notion of the frontier and a synecdoche of American national character. I would add that his places are not only American. There are, of course, seas and mountains all over the world, and living cities (and ruins) in India and China and everywhere else. Other settler societies like Canada, Argentina, and Brazil have frontiers in reality and imagined community myth.

The era after Whitman saw new commodities circulate in a global economy and this helped create a new lifestyle in places all over the world. This was when suburbia became established and when consumerism became a more important valence of status. This reaches its apotheosis in the post-World War Two era. Writing then, Lewis Mumford argues that the suburbs were:

> A multitude of uniform, unidentifiable houses, lined up inflexibly at uniform distances, on uniform roads, in a treeless communal waste, inhabited by people of the same

> class, the same income, the same age group, witnessing the same television performances, eating the same tasteless prefabricated foods, from the same freezers, conforming in every outward and inward respect to a common mould … The ultimate effect of the suburban escape in our own time is, ironically, a low-grade uniform environment from which escape is impossible.

Mumford's long opening sentence compounded by the rhetorical repetition, first of 'uniform' and then of 'same' before the final return of 'uniform', heightens the claim that suburbia is monotonous and boring as well as deracinated and alienated. His language of critique reflects the very prison he describes. The suburbanite is the one who cannot escape, the figure who is so indentured that they fail to apprehend the truth of the 'waste' and 'tastelessness' that is their life. It is the prison of our time, except, of course, for the actual prisons, refugee camps, and detention centres that are so numerous.

However, in thinking through the suburbs and responding to people like Mumford, I not only want to focus on contemporary content that is suburban, to simply read culture and rituals that are located there, but to also create a frame of reference in a language of my own making. The question is not: what is happening in the suburbs? But rather, how does a suburbanist think?

In that way, the suburbanist is the thinking subject who negates the Othering suburbanite. It is the political, aesthetic, familial individual who knows that their self is made by their connections, and, so to think, be, do as a suburbanist is to think, be, do as a citizen, a poet, and a sibling, parent, elder. They reclaim what is possible in the suburbs at the level of language, ecology, and social relations in order to see the truth of this place and its potential. Its aim is liberation from death where soft power tastes are made and elections are decided. This is important for a poetics that aims to connect with how the majority now live in the United States, Canada, and New Zealand, if not anywhere else there are gated communities, outlet malls and big box stores, and all the hallmarks of what make a suburban lifestyle. It is a truly global phenomenon.

As part of this global phenomenon, I recall my recent trip to Lulu Mall in Ernakalum in Kerala, south India. This is an hour away from where I was living at the time and two hours from my mother's ancestral village. I was there because I needed to do my shopping. Until that point in time I had been buying food from the local store up the road, riding my bike past the swaying coconut palms and the small plastic fires that pollute the air on the cusp of darkness. But, on the day of Donald Trump's election, demonetisation had been implemented in India, which meant that RS500 and RS1000 notes had been declared illegal tender by the national government. In a cash heavy economy, it affected people's daily habits in an irrevocable way.

For me, it meant catching an Uber to India's largest mall an hour away to stock up on food once a week rather than using my small denominations at the end of each workday. In this particular instance, it meant that the government had intervened to create the conditions in which I was encouraged to be stereotypically suburban in my shopping habits, precisely because other avenues of consumption were shut off due to the lack of credit card facilities and cash in ATMs. There are, of course, other discourses available to read this situation – 'modernisation' or 'late capitalism' or 'state intervention' in particular. But a supermarket in a mall in the developing world is as suburban a space as any.

Standing there as the fluorescent lights shone and the air conditioning blasted cool air, I thought of Allen Ginsberg's 'A Supermarket in California', written in Berkeley in 1955:

> What thoughts I have of you tonight Walt Whitman, for I walked down the sidestreets under the trees with a headache self-conscious looking at the full moon.
>
> In my hungry fatigue, and shopping for images, I went into the neon fruit supermarket, dreaming of your enumerations!

What peaches and what penumbras! Whole families shopping at night! Aisles full of husbands! Wives in the avocados, babies in the tomatoes! – and you, Garcia Lorca, what were you doing down by the watermelons?

I saw you, Walt Whitman, childless, lonely old grubber, poking among the meats in the refrigerator and eyeing the grocery boys.

I heard you asking questions of each: Who killed the pork chops? What price bananas? Are you my Angel?

I wandered in and out of the brilliant stacks of cans following you, and followed in my imagination by the store detective.

We strode down the open corridors together in our solitary fancy tasting artichokes, possessing every frozen delicacy, and never passing the cashier.

Where are we going, Walt Whitman? The doors close in an hour. Which way does your beard point tonight?

(I touch your book and dream of our odyssey in the supermarket and feel absurd.)

Will we walk all night through solitary streets? The trees add shade to shade, lights out in the houses, we'll both be lonely.

Will we stroll dreaming of the lost America of love past blue automobiles in driveways, home to our silent cottage?

Ah, dear father, graybeard, lonely old courage-teacher, what America did you have when Charon quit poling his ferry and you got out on a smoking bank and stood watching the boat disappear on the black waters of Lethe?

The stream-of-consciousness voice with its flowing, lyrical, run on lines remind me of *Leaves of Grass*. Yet Ginsberg's playful, ironic tone is contrapuntal to Whitman's earnest and celebratory mode. Other scholars have read 'A Supermarket in California' as a document of America, of the West, of food, of libido, of drugs, of history, of the Classics, and of the market, emphasising Ginsberg's particular relationship to the senior poet. Although 'A Supermarket in California' can be read in these ways, it also participates in closing the era that Whitman envisioned and opening out to a new consumer identity that was a song of a self refracted through goods of creative destruction and inbuilt obsolescence.

When Ginsberg wrote this poem in 1955, there was a historic change in how Americans were living. This was suburbanism. In other words, Minerva's owl had flown from modernity and Modernism too – this was the precise moment when Americans were consumed by a lifestyle ethos. Neon and frozen foods were relatively new commodities that brought with them an idea of the future; automobiles dominated; and 'the people' now lived in silent cottages. Ginsberg's 'queerying', penultimate question is of the suburban and speaks directly to consumerism as a function of American identity. It speaks of the car, that vehicle of freedom, the frontier, the West, as being stationary – it is still like Whitman's feet, its dreams grounded in the everyday prison of concrete, tarmac and box home that was the new reality of post-war America.

But, in a quality less remarked upon, the poem also reaches for the transnational – citing Frederico Garcia Lorca to ask of him 'what were you doing down by the watermelons?' Of course, watermelons circulate in a raced context in the American imagination and so they cannot be divorced from internal empire. But, they were also to be found outside the continental bounds, being native to southern Africa and first cultivated in Ancient Egypt. From Egypt, watermelons spread north through Europe and were planted in the Americas in the late 16th century, initially in Florida and then up the East Coast. James Cook brought them to Hawaii and the Pacific on his voyages two hundred years later. By the time the Japanese first grew seedless watermelons in 1939, the fruit was truly global. When coupled with the use of Lorca, arguably a world historical poetic martyr who brings to mind emotional ideas of an international Left, we know that Ginsberg's supermarket was the suburban space of consumption that contained new technologies found in other settler societies if not the world round. Supermarkets were a key part of that.

When Ginsberg was writing there were still rural enclaves in Appalachia and urban coteries in the Bay Area, just as there are today and on Trump's election day the week before I was shopping in demonetised India. In other words 'America' itself was not and is not singular even if we think this poem can be a synecdoche of the nation as a whole. We move from Whitman in the prototypically suburban state of New Jersey to Ginsberg on the Californian frontier of suburbanisation. This was exported across an increasingly American globe through the soft power visions of Hollywood and Madison Avenue, and the hard power of the military industrial complex. In this, we begin to see the contours of a lifestyle that extends the world over and that many still aspire to. This is the American dream, which in Ginsberg's estimation might be a nightmare. But, right now, is it only available in America and was it ever just a dream? That was the question I asked in Lulu Mall in Kerala, where the landscape and social relations are different and the modes of production cannot simply be exported to the peripheries of empires on the other side of the globe.

Standing in the deli section texting my wife on my iPhone 7, I asked whether I should use the joint account credit card to purchase Monterrey Jack cheese and a loaf of white bread in plastic wrap. In that moment, I thought of the after effects of globalisation, of what had been imported and exported and how we lived in an era of mass consumption. I wanted to ask of Ginsberg, as he asked of Whitman:

> Oh, dear father, ashen hair, bell-charmed howling preacher, what world did you have when McArthur quit commanding his frigates and you got out on the Left Bank and stood watching the smoke disappear from the frontier?

To see the suburbs now, and suburbanisation as a process, and suburbanism as a poetics, means thinking through what the place and consciousness of lifestyle enables. Does it necessitate seeing beyond the nation state? Does it mean coming into a clearer understanding of consumption as the ties that bind us? Does it mean finding the higher synthesis of the country and the city as a poetics that is dialectical? The short answer to each of those questions is 'yes'. But, the longer ones depend on how we define those things.

We know from the history of print culture, that poets often read outside their national bounds. This is not only in Ginsberg's engagement with 'the East', but there in minor figures like Rex Ingamells who kept a correspondence with poets all over the globe from his base in suburban Melbourne during the same era. The answer to the first question of seeing beyond the nation state also involves understanding what signs we traffic in – a poem about McDonalds, like Kanye West's 'Untitled' in the magazine *Boys Don't Cry*, circulates in a world that could be labeled American in one language game but is also a suburban trope from a global economy that is post-statist. We could speak here of the Big Mac Index from *The Economist* as well as the fast food public sphere which is multinational if quite islanded.

This brings us to the second question, where we can think through the idea of consumption as a way to understand identity. This means complementing identities that are established, particularly those grounded in the body and its modes of production – 'franchise laborer' or 'area manager' or 'chief executive officer' is more readily understood than 'McNugget eater'. In addition, the identities of consumption are located in specific actions rather than in the collective entrainments of being. In any case, it means restoring a conversation about consumption to how we see ourselves in the suburbs – whether we are defined by shopping at Walmart rather than a farmer's market; whether someone becomes suburban when they wear Nike Air Max but not Gucci loafers; whether your shopping determines what group you belong to as much as your job.

These two responses, as the material basis for a poetics, means dwelling on the last proposition and trying to find the suburbs as a higher synthesis of the city and the country, as a distinct lifestyle that is being performatively enunciated. This means thinking through location beyond the nation. The suburbs are truly worldwide rather than simply American. After all, one can find manifestations of the suburbs in distinct locations – Lulu Mall in Ernakalum is only one place but there are gated compounds with do-it-yourself builders in Barranco and freeways for gas guzzling cars along the Garden Route. In our language games these places can either be named more specifically, down to the number of the street, or more generally, up to the state they are categorised within. For example, we might say that Lulu Mall is in Edapally as well as India, but it is a dialogic process to know whether or not the audience understands those points of reference. This is the realisation that the place exists in a network that can always be edited and so if the interpretive lens is infinite so too are the sources and implications. Understanding poetry about that might help us understand who we are and what we have become since Whitman wrote of the suburbs all those years before. That might be the task of the suburbanist who simply wants to go shopping at the local vegetable stand after a day at work.

6

The Next Suburb Over

There is a continual thread of thoughtful reflection that connects the suburbs to Australian national identity. It is one that harks back, in particular, to a discursive moment just after the Second World War, when suburbia as a demographic reality and set of lifestyle choices sprawled into new territory. The 1950s was 'the suburban moment'. This is seen when writers like Donald Horne and Robyn Boyd expressed a mood of intellectual despair a decade later, and took evident pleasure in negating this new common man. They, and others, were reflecting on sudden material changes, on how the car, television, bungalow became the norm, when Australia lost something fundamental in its suburbanisation. And yet, the 1950s boom and its 1960s detractors, provide a bedrock for thinking about 'character' and how that connects to poetic, and other cultural, expressions of 'Australianness' now. After all, suburban Australia is there wherever we look: in cinema with *The BBQ* (2018); in painting with the Howard Arkley retrospective at Tarrawarra in 2016; in television with a wide selection of reality shows including *Married At First Sight*; on the nightly broadcast news that advertises crime on the peripheries of what constitutes our parochial centres; in music with Courtney Barnett's *Depreston* (2016). The suburbs are a perennial topic for culture and hence public debate in Australia, but they are so present that they remain undefined, an absent centre that becomes a calcified assumption. In the common sense language games of today, quite simply, you know the suburbs when you see them.

As they are normally understood, the suburbs are places between the urban and the rural, places that bisect 'Sydney and the bush', a site between the Athenian/Boeotian as Les Murray would have it. Ludwig Wittgenstein echoes a common theme when he defined them as 'a multitude of new boroughs with straight regular streets and uniform houses.' They are the conformist and planned buildings recently added to the city and encroaching on nature. This is not the new in the modernist dictum 'to make it new', nor is it to *epater les bourgeois*. Rather, it is a simple material condition of coming after the city and even later than the country. We could infer that they are simulacra, facsimile, fake. They are second order versions of the culture found in the metropole, fresh from the packet with new commodities that are fetishes thanks to invasive forms of advertising. And in so doing, suburbs displace wildness, colonise landscapes, and occupy ecologies.

But the suburbs do speak back to such assumptions, being home to all kinds of people, being home to older buildings, being home to trees that provide refuge for migrating birds, to say nothing of the possums one gets in the roof come winter. In the Australian imagination, they are also the site for a relaxed if not comfortable eccentricity from Dame Edna Everage to *Kath & Kim* to Dale Kerrigan. We often read the suburbs as neither here nor there, caught in between in a negative way. They have none of the frisson of the metropolitan and lack the vibrancy of opera, galleries, and stadiums. But they are also without the possibility of nature's majestic calm, let alone the rejuvenating power of wide-open space that generates the sublime within us. The suburbs fail because they are not one thing or another. And yet, they have the possibility of being a perfect marriage precisely because they can be a mediation of the country and the city, a place to dwell in, not merely to pass through.

At its most basic, suburbia suggests a *lifestyle*, a way of life that is shaped by class but not defined by it. There are middle class suburbs, working class suburbs, rich suburbs, but they are all suburbs at the end of the day. Lifestyle, after all, is a catchall word I have heard at backyard barbeques in the phrases 'it's just such a great lifestyle' and 'we moved here for the lifestyle'. It is even buried in the ignominious Tony Abbott sound bite 'lifestyle choices'. When people are asked to unpack it, they tend to suggest pragmatic definitions – schools, housing prices, public transport – thinking through the infrastructural necessities of daily life. They might also unconsciously mean lifestyle in the way Max Weber used it when he wrote:

> The chances of attaining social honor are primarily determined by differences in the *styles of life* ... social honor very frequently and typically is associated with the respective stratum's legally guaranteed and monopolised claim to sovereign rights or to income and profit opportunities of a certain kind. Thus, if all characteristics are found, which, of course, is not always the case a 'status group' is a group societalised through its special *styles of life*, its conventional and specific notions of honor, and the economic opportunity it monopolises.

In this passage, we see the connection of lifestyle to status, social honour, income, prestige, rights and education. And so, lifestyle becomes 'intersectional' and we must recognise that it matters over and above one valence of identity like race or class or gender.

At this stage, lifestyle consciousness is not the national consciousness of an imagined community or an awareness grounded in the relationship between labour and capital. We cannot speak of it in the same way as 'class consciousness'. But, a more developed concept of lifestyle may equip commentators to think beyond the cultural cringe, liberal identity politics, and even a reversion to class as the definition of population differences. Indeed, it's not absurd to suggest that suburbia offers distinct ways of being in the world. Suburbanites are not 'inner city elites' or 'country bumpkins' and in the everyday living that happens in the suburbs, we might come to understand something beyond liberalism and its rhetoric. It can offer a cohesive form of group identity that is nevertheless grounded in materialist reality.

Of course, lifestyles between individuals differ as much as suburbs differ from one to another. *Neighbours*' Erinsborough is not the same as *Home and Away*'s Summer Bay in the fictional landscape, let alone similar to my Wembley, a suburb of Perth in Western Australia. Although Erinsborough, Summer Bay and Wembley are unique, the suburbs are a global phenomenon. The ties of lifestyle that bind them together include fast fashion and branded gadgets, recognisable cars and flat pack furniture. In our own time, the attributes, component parts, ideals of the suburbs are archipelagic if not multinational.

But, the suburbs find a particular expression in Australia. Peter Timms casts suburbia as a foundational settler myth in *Australia's Quarter Acre*:

> Although in its early years, the settlement at Sydney Cove was little more than a slave farm for criminals, there were those with the foresight to imagine a brighter future for it … Their dream of a new democratic society, young, healthy and classless, found its clearest expression in the notion of suburbs, where all citizens would have the opportunity to form communities, express their creativity and make themselves useful. From the very beginning, suburbia was at the heart of Australia's self-identity.

Timms gives us a celebratory definition of some of the virtues of suburbia – democratic, young, healthy, classless, creative, useful. These are qualities that could be therapeutic for the jailed even as it forgets the myths of *terra nullius* and colonial displacement. And that is one way to read the animating spirit of the emerging society down under. But, if the suburbs have been at the heart of settler Australia since the eighteenth century, and cause for occasional celebration, critics have long maligned them as well.

For the 'thinking Australian', the suburbs are often boring, deracinated, and dull. This is particularly the case for post-war commentators who wrote during the era of mass suburbanisation under Robert Menzies. Together, they mocked the dullness of the ordinary monoculture of most Australian neighbourhoods. As their contemporary Ronald Taft stated:

> Australia has had up to three adult generations in which a substantial part of the population could be caricatured as 8.10 am train catchers, Saturday gardeners and do-it-yourself home improvers, local school, sporting, social, fraternal and church club stalwarts and, in more recent years, indulgers in the remote-control togetherness of reading the same newspapers and receiving the same radio and TV programmes as their neighbours. Today, 80 per cent of all Australian big city dwellers live in detached single-family houses, nearly all wholly or partially owned by the occupier, and nearly all with some type of private garden.

Taft saw suburbia as a style of life over and above work or leisure or religion or property or landscape alone. His portrait of the Australian majority in the mid-century is an outline that doesn't quite correspond to how we live today, not least in regards to home-ownership and church attendance, and perhaps with the rise of watch on demand, 'remote-control togetherness'. Yet, we can use this historical view of the suburbs as a way to connect with a truer image of what Australia now is. We can establish the facts of ordinary lives rather than entrench the intellectual myths of the post-war nation. In so doing we can reclaim something from 1950s suburban Australia to develop a contemporary poetics.

Today, the suburbs offer country living, city benefits. They hold out a way of being that promises a higher realisation of both those archetypal places. In Australia, the bush myth matters and so too does the urban, but the suburbs are where 'the people' live. They decide our elections from Western Sydney to the Gold Coast corridor. They decide our popular culture from *Masterchef* to *Survivor*. They decide our public media debate from refugees to climate change. If only *SBS World News* or *Q&A* had the ratings of the commercial news. The suburbs are where hearts and minds are won. They matter for what they are and the power they have.

Although mid-century intellectuals have mainly left a legacy of suburban derision, their observations opened up an opportunity. As Max Harris wrote in 1963:

> Australians live in an enormous suburbia, the variations of which are matters of income and affluence rather than manners and values. Between Vaucluse and Paddington manners and mores vary only in affluence and sophistication, not in kind. Australian society is bleakly uniform. There is even, in the tribal sense, no real proletariat in Australia and this, at the very heart of things, explains the post-war moral dissolution of the Australian Labor Party. The ALP still subsumes the existence of a class-conscious proletariat tribally different from the middle and entrepreneurial class. There are trade unions, income variations, occupational hierarchies, but no clear-cut differentiation of *living patterns*. The wharfie in a Port Melbourne pub would have been hard put to 'pick' Essington Lewis [the industrialist] in the saloon bar by virtue of his accent, reactions, stance or presence. The social homogenousness of Australian life means that trade unionists unconsciously think of themselves as an economic pressure group, but not as a special social class.

In observing 'living patterns', Harris' claim offers an entry point for a contemporary language that might be responsive to suburban Australia. After all, shifting the suburbs as a type of lifestyle to the centre of conversation offers the opportunity to realign our frames of reference. The suburbs are not simply for 'ordinary Australians' 'working families' or 'battlers': they are their own type of ecology and social relations. They offer something different and distinct, and lifestyle consciousness offers a way of being holistic that does not solely depend on an economic identity. Recall Weber: status, social honour, income, prestige, rights, and education. Recall your neighbour or your cousin or that blokey stranger at the backyard barbeque: schools, public transport, coffee shops, sporting facilities, and hospitals.

And so, it is an ongoing task to raise the consciousness of the lifestyle majority, to articulate what is actually happening in places where most Australians now live. Since Harris was writing, there has been a precipitous decline in union membership, a shift towards consumer identity, the harsh reality of a globalised free trade economy, the private-public partnerships common to universities, the rise of feminist involvement in the economic and public sphere, and the openings offered up by conversations about identity. Australia has changed immeasurably since White, Horne, Boyd, Taft and Harris wrote, and so have the suburbs.

To think through that, we must let go of the nostalgia for inner city neighbourhoods that were industrial centres and pivot to the suburbs proper. Vincent Buckley's analysis seems prescient today:

> Certainly, there is a steady drift from suburbia, in one sense. In Melbourne, the young married lecturer who ten years ago would have considered it inevitable to go to a six roomed timber villa in Cheltenham or Box Hill might now think first of Carlton, Parkville or even North Melbourne, places which in time may even become the suburban fringes of the university. But in this, too, they are not untypical of the society as a whole, the slow drift back towards the city has been joined by a variety of middle-class types. The fact is, that these inner-suburban areas are ceasing to be industrial centres and slums. So a preference for Carlton over Kew may be as bourgeois a piece of conformism as any other. In either place, his neighbours are likely to think of the university man as very much like themselves – engaged in a different 'job', certainly, and doing it in the uniform of tweed jacket and slacks rather than a dark suit which is mandatory elsewhere but giving himself no airs and pretending to the appropriate trade-skills rather than to any special sources of enlightenment.

> Obviously there are advantages as well as disadvantages in this conformity to national habit; but one cannot be expected to welcome the phenomenon with much enthusiasm.

Buckley may well be describing the gentrification of the inner city in our own time, the place where a bourgeoisie goes for cold drip coffee rather than saving pennies for a house and backyard an hour's drive away to places where they are only just beginning to ride the brioche-bun, burger wave. If 'the suburbs' are a cave, the inner city is simply another one deeper still, which is why suburbs matter to Australia as a whole or to the archipelagos all over the world. And when we look here, look at ourselves in a global context next to Bombay and Patagonia, we will see that we have very little that is urban and very little that is frontier. Welcome to the suburbs. Welcome to Australia.

*

In particular, I can imagine a more complete suburbanism in my field of poetry. A conflict over Australian identity and poetry was revealed in the conversation around Puncher & Wattman's *Anthology of Contemporary Australian Poetry*. The split emerged between traditional verse culture proponents who bemoaned the absence of bush ballads and members of avant-gardes resistant to the very idea of the nation. In other words, this was the country versus the city. According to critics like David Campbell, representing the first group, and Corey Wakeling, representing the second, the anthology neglected both their respective constituencies. The response echoed the division between Les Murray and John Tranter from a previous generation.

These polar criticisms may yield a higher ground, in the form of a theory of the suburban. In the most immediate way, the *Anthology* included poems of suburban spaces, including Luke Beesley's 'Split in the Table', Pam Brown's 'Authentic Local', Lachlan Brown's 'Evensong', Judith Bishop's 'T/here' and Diane Fahey's 'In the House'. They each present a view of the suburbs that comes after Bruce Dawe and Gwen Harwood, a contemporary critique and celebration of significant spaces, putting paid to any notion that it is only Athens and Boeotia that we need to choose from. That divide from Murray forgets all of Asia Minor.

The suburban interrupts both the frontier myths of Murray and Campbell and the bright lights of Tranter and Wakeling. In that way, the new poetry of suburbia collected in the Puncher & Wattman *Anthology* can engage with suburban lifestyles, and present new responses to old criticisms of them. Although we surely benefit from both poetries, we do not need to choose between the Banjo Paterson Australian Poetry Festival in Orange (Annual) or the *Active Aesthetics* Conference on Australian Poetry in Berkeley (2016). We can probably go to each one, but maybe we can just go to our local coffee shop to listen to someone from the Australian Poetry Café Poet Program (2009–2014). That was on high streets in suburbs wherever poets dwell, that was where we can find a poetics of suburbanism.

We might think of the suburbanist's worldview as a kind of synthetic poetic sensibility that comes from suburban space but is the negation of the suburbanite. In that way the poet is not only called into the role as a bard of suburbia per se. Rather, it is that the poet has the potential to express the true consciousness of lifestyle in a way that articulates what has been happening on these islands since at least the post-war era. The responsibility may be bardic in that they are held up to be the voice of their people but that would rely on their being a suburban identity to begin with, which means thinking through what a grounding in country and a local culture looks like in our contemporary age when the Census organises us by postcode. Needless to say, a true poetic consciousness is one that is critical and engaged, calling forth an enlightened notion of what it is to be from and for a place, one that negates the suburbanite exploitation of the material base without a dialectical care in the world for recycling, parent and teacher meetings, and the community hall where life takes place.

*

John Coetzee wrote on Les Murray's idea of 'sprawl' for the *New York Review of Books* in 2011:

> One of the chief Australian values that he celebrates is sprawl. Sprawl is to Murray what loafing is to Whitman: an at-easeness in the world that upsets the tidy minds of schoolteachers and urban planners. 'Reprimanded and dismissed/sprawl,' 'listens with a grin and one boot up on the rail/of possibility.'

As endearing and rebellious as Coetzee's shorthand representation may seem, 'sprawl' should not simply be glossed as 'at easeness'. In Murray's poem 'The Quality of Sprawl', it is a type of inventiveness (the Rolls Royce cut into an ute), an approximation (farming 'roughly'), a generosity (driving hitchhikers), a frugality unable to be bought ('never lighting cigars with ten–dollar notes'), a bit of luck, the rub of the green, the leftover or extra (bananas, in this case), 'the fifteenth to the twenty-first lines in a sonnet', classlessness, 'not throwing up' in a neighbour's bed, 'an image of my country', and 'roughly Christian'. It is not: 'Society', it is 'not harming the official', not 'brutality', 'Simon de Montfort', 'lewd advances; 'hitting animals' or 'speeding'.

In this way, Murray yokes sprawl to an idea of his place, which is, in his own words Bunyah as a specific Australian rural town with roots in Christianity as well as a projective synecdoche that matters beyond itself. Yet, it also connects us to class, proposing that it is classless, which forgets the necessity of being aware of the proletariat, modes of production, and alienation. It is unable to see what might be achieved when one enters more fully into the particularity of a lifestyle identity.

As useful as this poetic identification of what sprawl is, it might be necessary to see how it functions in our common understanding of space. To dirempt Murray's poetics from the ordinary language of sprawl itself suggests that poetry is separate from everyday speech, including that of the political economy. This is not the case when it simultaneously relies on a social observation and animating antagonisms that are grounded in those very same, very political formations. After all, sprawl is what we think of when we think of cities, how they are expanding from the CBD into places that Murray might be said to represent, belong to and write of. Our suburbs are 'sprawling' into new territories and this term is often meant as a derogatory one that speaks to the failings of new place making. This holds despite the fact that people live there and the real estate housing industrial complex would have Australians believe that the quarter acre is still the dream. It does not need to be so, we do not need sprawl to have an 'at easeness' such as Coetzee would have us read into Murray, and we do not need sprawl as a way of occupying land that is our shared border.

To think too, of sprawl in the country at our bush block in Redgate where the subdivisions on farming land are coming down the road from Witchcliffe. With that there are re-routed creeks, removed trees, occupied public space. This has implications for me personally but it also presents new challenges for the changing face of the constituency Murray seems to represent. Redgate is not Bunyah, but I do not mind if it becomes Wembley. We cannot promote an Australia where ecologies are destroyed simply because we seek a largesse, seek a lifestyle that is so focused on consumption in an age of global economics, and for that reason, we might think of how to disagree with 'sprawl' as a poetic quality and a political formation.

But, in critiquing Murray, we cannot simply forget about the other side of the debate, folding ourselves into an experimental avant-garde that champions some rootless cosmopolitan metropole against the country as it were. In that way, the pure negation of sprawl complicates modernist ideas that poets need to make it new. New houses, like new poetic experiments, are sprawl from the cities of sonnets, haiku, villanelles after all.

We might oppose sprawl with the *retrofitting* of suburban spaces in order to balance both our poetry and our politics. It is important for re-tooling progressive ideas of Australia from the re-discovery of the archive that would suggest we have a poetic tradition to be proud of right here on this continent to the solar panels currently being added to old suburbs.

Retrofitting means overcoming an unnecessary fetish for the new while at the same time sensing the possibilities that come with being truly here in a place with spirits and land that is old as well. But, it might not be about making them part of a modernist lineage, not thinking of them in critical terms as if they are avant-garde. They are, as far as I can tell, not structural interventions in the field of 'the new'. This might mean encouraging a kind of suburbanism instead, one that leans contemporary. It does not immediately follow that we cannot see it as part of a contemporary critique of the nation itself.

These are not the only possibilities either. The suburbanist might want to take attentiveness to embodiment and combine it with formal innovation. The suburbanist might want to champion the marginalised with an international frame of reference. The suburbanist might want to advocate for defamiliarised everyday speech aware of a digital sensibility. No matter what they choose though, we cannot turn away from the suburban. In it we can seek an understanding of who we are beyond being simple inheritors of a romantic or modernist tradition. A suburbanism based on a retrofitted poetics finds a higher synthesis between the country and the city as they were personified by an earlier generation of poets. And that surely, is about expanding what is possible and paying respect to our past through developing a true consciousness of a lifestyle shared by the majority here and millions more who live all over the globe.

In looking back at the suburban moment in Australian intellectual culture from the 1950s, the reader could be forgiven for thinking that there is nothing in there to be proud of. But we find in these negations of the ordinary, a possibility that poets can work with in our own time. We can find in them a rich compost and neon light that heats us and shines ever brighter. From that, we might begin to understand our own present in a language of our own making that speaks about what belonging is with a truthfulness of the human condition in the most basic sense. That might be what a suburbanist poetics offers to us right here, right now, as we begin to think of who we are and why we matter to the world at large.

INTERLUDE

Suburbanist 6014

I grew up in the western suburbs of Boorloo/Perth in Wembley, 6014. There are things that I experienced there that many other people experienced in their own postcodes. This is not to assume that these experiences belong to any nation or city or country in particular. Suburban forms of belonging are suburban and should be thought of that way, first and foremost. After all, my world is a world of suburbs, and, my suburbanism is a part of a new worldly literature. Being from Wembley means being from, about and for those suburbs, and, working to make them into a new kind of lifestyle.

The suburbanism I have learnt suggests how we can live with joy, clarity and respect through a poetic consciousness that articulates, celebrates and reflects our daily lives. This does not mean we should ignore the alienation, exploitation and injustice of these places. It does not mean we can gloss over the realities of colonialism, capitalism, racism, and a whole host of other ills. It means we must work together to make poetry from the moments when the birds and frogs sing and croak, when the alarm goes off and the coffee pot drips louder than before, when the commuters on the train platforms crowd and swell.

We must live inside that before we begin to write about the meaning of our homes. We must be suburbanists who see the truth of our worlds. This is about expressing ourselves in the language games that allows us to become enlightened. Enlightenment nowadays might not happen under a Bodhi tree or in a cave, but on a lawn made lush by summer rain or on a bridge between home and hospital or over a cup of tea with views of the sea. Wembley, and other suburbs, can be a place of this as much as anywhere else, and, to think as much of this means repatriation, uncolonising, and desettling. This matters for living a poetic life even if you are lost and the working day is long and you never have enough time to yourself. My vision of a poetic life is what follows in this mosaic of my childhood in Wembley. It is from a time before the quarter acre blocks had been carved up for duplexes, before the old trees had been cut down, before the video store had closed. This is not to be nostalgic. My home suburb still has beautiful homes, migrating birds, and ways to spend time together. But, it is to frame it in a certain point in time, to reflect on Wembley as a place as good as any other, and, to examine the past of a particular suburb with the aim of reinvigorating the future of many more.

*

The way the icing sits atop the cake, the point where it meets, not a skin, not an impression, not a barrier, but a mixing of the two into a third. It happens for chocolate, lemon poppy, sponge. This detail matters at the primary school bake sale where they are raising money for cancer, for heart attacks, for spina bifida. It is the kind of thing people overlook, but it is the thing that determines what cake you buy with your pocket money. This is the taste that lingers in the mouth, not a madeleine, not a meat pie, but the place where cake meets icing. You find it in other places, this mixing, and in some way, it is all mixing, all the time, no matter how you look at it. Mixing, beautiful mixing, icing on cake, the colour of sprinkles bleeding into the white.

*

Over our back fence there is a swimming pool. Our cousins have one a couple of suburbs over, too. When you fly above you can see them dotting the suburbs blue. We play 'Marco Polo' – someone calls with their eyes closed, we respond, and they try to corner us, a kind of blind chasey in the swimming pool. I do not think about who Marco Polo is, or whether they play 'Dirk Hartog' in Venice, let alone 'Yagan' in Paris. Or why we love this game so much. At other times, we just make a splash, or stand on boogie boards, or throw a tennis ball until we get bored. No matter where you go, there are always honeysuckle flowers in the pool, and small leaves from the same bushes, even if the bushes themselves are nowhere to be seen. No one knows their origin, no one knows why and how and when they come to be here. When they float in the pool, we cup them in our hands, like bees with water clogged wings, and put them on the dry ground. In the distance, we can see the bore water stains on the outside walls of the houses where our friends and cousins live. It is the same colour as the rotted honeysuckles that are everywhere.

*

In the morning before school, I sit with my grandfather reading the paper. We do not speak, not even to point out what is interesting, and he stares at the pages intensely, his dark skin shiny with coconut oil. I watch him watching the world as it comes to him, this way. They have alarming headlines here, and it is different to his experience with *The Straits Times*, which he read for so many years. We read and do not speak. We make our way through the news of the day, together, thinking about what the famine, the bombing, the drought mean to us here, so far away in this suburb. And all we can think about is what we can do for those people, about how we cannot forget the people we left behind, who are all family somehow, somewhere, and the ones we have come to be with here, in this new place we are learning to belong to.

*

At the end of my street is a lake. There is a nature centre where they host talks and birdwatching events for all the migratory species that stop off on journeys elsewhere. They tell us to watch out for tiger snakes and if we see them we should not touch them. Some kids come and play here after school. They wade through the bulrushes with bare feet and don't get scared when they see the snakes swimming towards them. Sometimes, we just come and watch the geese and the pelicans and the reed warblers and the finches and the egrets and the swans and the eagles and the herons and the magpies and the owls. We sit there and point them out to each other, but we cannot label them, cannot name them according to what others call them. We describe them to each other, say what one looks like and where it might be coming from. We think about them as things of beauty and of wonder, of how they are visitors here, just like us, and the lake laps at our feet, making our toes wet before dinner.

*

At the other end of my street is the food court. I love it as much as anywhere else. It is almost home cooking. My grandparents come from Singapore to live with us and we go there to eat noodles – laksa, char kway teow, mee hoon from the local hawker stand. They have soybean milk too, not as fresh as the one my grandparents would get back home in Seletar Hills but good enough to take the sting out of the chilli when they add too much. We talk about the food that we want to eat, food we miss as they do – popiah and chendol, mangosteen and rambutan. My dad always talks about how there are so few bananas here, how in other places you can get ones to go with putu, ones to eat in a single mouthful, any kind of banana, just for the right occasion. And the food court feels like someone's kitchen because we sit there and say hi to our friends and the people who go there, the regulars who make the place what it is. But they do not have enough bananas, not for us, and we try to remember what they taste like as far away as we are.

*

It is local council elections again and we are walking through Wembley. Our whole family is out together and we are walking all weekend, and some school day evenings, dropping leaflets into letterboxes to support our candidate. We are citizens after all, and so, we want to put our best foot forward, regardless if there are problems with the governance of this place.

We vote for the person who is going to put more money into the school, who is going to look after the old people, who is going to make the park better, who is going to give out the best books at the end of year assembly when they reward the students who have done well. We want them to be like us – people who love our suburb. They need to cheer us when we play Floreat Park in soccer, or when Subiaco comes over to debate us, or when we have to choose which high school to go to because Wembley does not have one, not yet, anyhow. We want a local councilor who has veggies in their backyard (chickens are a bonus), who does not have a fancy car, who watches sport on the weekend, who eats sausages in white bread, who might even play *Street Fighter*. And so, we walk kilometers and kilometers, back and forth, stuffing leaflets into letterboxes next to catalogues of white goods, next to food coupons, next to real estate agent's calendars. And, then we wait for election night, to see what will happen, hoping that we did enough to get them over the line.

*

Wembley is the main island in my childhood archipelago, but on the weekend we make our way to others all over Perth. We do not know the right names to call these places, the ones that make sense for the country that these suburbs sit atop. It is stolen land, and, to think that the lifestyle here is what people live for. We know that we are on Whadjuk land and are at school with Nyoongar friends, but these suburbs have a different tongue, a deeper one. We play sport everywhere and our club takes us to what we call Girrawheen, Kingsley, Cockburn, Kelmscott, Joondalup. We travel for hours looking out the windows wearing our uniforms wondering whether we will win or lose or draw, wondering what these other suburbs are like, whether they have bake sales and fetes and wetlands. Sometimes we go to places and the other team will all be from the same motherland – Scotland, Vietnam, Italy, South Africa, Chile. Rarely, they are like us with people from everywhere, including this place where we stand. But, we love soccer and footy and tennis and basketball and hockey, and we play it until the season is over. Every time, we get a trophy and the coach will say something nice even if we had more losses than not. We will go and eat ice cream, and the next sport will start the weekend after. And then, like always, on every Saturday, we will drive from Wembley to other suburbs where we want to belong just like others.

*

I am allowed to watch half an hour of commercial television per week and all the news I can stomach. The tv was never on in the morning and I had to choose my show carefully. Sometimes I would watch the same show for a few months in a row, but normally, I changed what I watched every single week. That meant I had a vague understanding of lots of shows but no idea what everyone was talking about when they gossiped at school. I like hearing people talk about *The Simpsons* or *The Fresh Prince of Bel Air* or *Saved by the Bell*. But, I am not curious to watch them myself. I like watching the news. Sometimes I sneak in the last ten minutes of *Wheel of Fortune* while my grandfather has a whiskey before dinner. Then, we settle in to hear about the world out there. It is so big, it is so far away, it is a place I will go to, someday.

*

Some weekends we go to the Swan River, that Derbarl Yerrigan. We sit on the banks of Matilda Bay and watch the birds, or scoop jellyfish and throw them at one another. Sometimes, we take a picnic, and go prawning at night, wearing old sandshoes and dragging a net behind, boiling the prawns right then and there, and, eating them fresh with lemon. The Swan River is always there for us. We see dolphins in it, and, go sailing by ourselves. My cousins and I are young, but we can handle small boats, race against other people and wear lifejackets and sunscreen and hats soaked through with sweat and water. The river seems to listen, to give life to the people around us, and we can see the buildings of the city in the distance.

At night, the lights reflect on the water. The skyscrapers are flashing their red and white lights, a world closed off from the fish and the midges and the figs, but they loom there, spectral and central all at once. And the river does not seem to care. It keeps flowing like it always has, and, we hope to help keep it alive through another year.

*

By the time Book Week comes around, we have forgotten what we had planned to go as at the end of the last one. Sometimes we help mum make our costumes and sometimes we co-ordinate with friends about going together. One year, my sister goes as the Tinman from the *Wizard of Oz* and is covered with foil that blows off in the wind. There are always lots of people dressed as Wally from *Where's Wally?* There are plenty of pirates and wizards and sports people. The size of the crowd that come to watch us parade around the quadrangle depends on the weather. People stand and take photos, and we pretend not to notice how embarrassing all our parents are, pretend not to smile at how proud they are that we read. We celebrate all the books that ever were. At assembly, the principal announces the awards and is dressed like a Teddy Bear.

*

They are logging the old growth forests in the South West, on Minang, Kaneang, and Pibelman country. We go down there for holidays and to visit family friends. We care about that placce, and so we march, just like thousands of others. We march to stop them from breaking it into a thousand pieces, to make sure the birds and the possums and the kangaroos have a place to rest and go, to eat and sleep, to be and simply live. We catch the bus from Wembley to march from the city to parliament. We let the government know that we will vote it out of power unless they keep the forests and safeguard it. And, in due course, we will win and logging there will become a thing of the past, if only for a moment. On that day, my mum will remind us that we helped a little bit, that we were part of people power. 'This is what it is to be a citizen' she will say and we will nod our heads like it truly matters.

*

We go and watch sport every now and then. One year, we get season tickets to the Perth Wildcats, and watch basketball that passes for professional. There we chant and they make a go of entertaining us. Other times, we watch the swimming world championships, which are not far from our house, and we point out the stars that we know from television. They look bigger in real life. One year, we go to watch West Perth play in the WAFL grand final. In the third quarter, there is a streaker and the security guards struggle to chase him down. When they tackle him, he is laughing and waving his jumper over his head. The crowd is screaming and clapping, they are enjoying the distraction, and the beer in their hands is thrown into the air. It is sunny and our dad cares because his childhood team will win the cup. But, it seems like the end of the league because a national one is being set up. We will remember it fondly – how the late afternoon sunlight makes the green of the oval shine bright, like they are playing on a disc of gold.

*

We raise money for charities – sometimes we sell chocolate, sometimes we jump rope, sometimes we go on fun runs. Every year, we run around Lake Monger, at the eastern edge of Wembley, where there are black swans and cygnets and palms. We line up and when we complete our lap, there is a sausage sizzle and balloons and a band to greet us. We rest and eat oranges. We talk with one another about how our time was faster than last year. And people laze on the grass and the principal makes a speech thanking us for raising money. The bowls club on the hill in the distance is standing sentinel. It seems like it has always belonged yet has never been there at all.

It used to be market gardens, an old man says, and hunting grounds. And the runners make their way home, going to the four corners of Wembley, and beyond, without a thought for the day that has just passed.

*

When we go to the beach, we go to City Beach. The waves come and go, like waves do, and we duck-dive and swim, get knocked over, build sand castles, walk up and down looking for other kids to play with. The day grows long and we slow somewhat. And then we run around until we cannot. The beach is a magnet for us six months of the year, and in the other six, we still come and visit, play in the playground on the grass, watch the sun set into the water and point to the clouds that are pink and orange and purple, wonder aloud when the stars will come out. And then we go home and fall asleep with salt in our hair, sand on our feet. The beach will be there tomorrow and the day after that and the day after that as well.

*

On Thursdays, there was a weekly assembly. They would hoist the flag; say the Lord's Prayer; hand out awards for tidying up and sport and music. I think about this, watch what goes on with distance, and question it. The last assembly I went to was on my last day of primary school. They gave me a certificate and a book that they think will serve me well. It is *Bulfinches Mythology* and I dip into it every now and then. I think about Icarus, and if he could have flown too close to the sun and fallen. But instead of dying, his father, Daedalus, catches him. He learns his lesson and they thank the gods by roasting meat and sprinkling water on offerings. They return to the village and dine out on that story for the rest of their lives. But that is a different story. That is a new myth that helps one live for days when the myths we know are not enough.

*

There used to be a rock-climbing gym on the border of Wembley and Jolimont, right next to a disused light industrial area that became a gated community of townhouses. They say in rock climbing, that you should have three points of contact. You need four – poetry, people, place, belief – and so, if you come off the rock, you know you will not fall. But, that is only if you are climbing without a rope. Climb with a rope instead. You might be able to save some others who you see falling. That might be what it is to have a heart and a home. That might be what it is to rock climb in the suburbs of memory for tomorrow.

PART TWO

7

The Poet in Suburbia

To the critic, suburbia seems to be a vast, elaborate, cruel system made up of individuals who are atomised, isolated, anonymous parts of a dull, monotonous, conformist machine. Standing in the metropolitan city or the pastoral countryside, the critic sees anyone who lives in the suburbs as an unthinking worshipper of false idols, a fool given over to caprice and lust, a capitalist sinner so antithetical to the real way of life that they are consigned to the trash-heap of forgetting.

To the critic, suburbia is worthless except for the guilty pleasures their taste desires, be that reality television, discounted fast food, or mass spectator sports. The critic rides on the coattails of the suburban system but always makes his displeasure known, always desiring to be subversive. When presented with a roast chicken he announces to all within earshot 'I am not hungry'. When a declaration of war is made, no matter the cause or the situation, be it national security or terrorism or personal safety, he announces to the assembled crowd 'I will not hurt a fly'. When the state asks him to vote he scorns the ballot box, claiming that no practical person could indeed be ethical, shouting from the rooftops 'I do not agree with the state' all the while collecting his cheque from the dole office, the public university, or the civil service.

This is the critic today, the one who has such righteous self-regard as to see himself as the moral voice of a generation, willing away his lust for commodities (books especially) and denigrating the audience he so crucially wishes to convert to his cause, and failing to think through 'the system' that suburbia and he are both implicated within. This critic feels like he must separate himself from 'the people' in dress, diet, politics, manners, comportment. His work should do this for him and he should find sympathy with those who struggle with death like he does. But he does not, he 'resists'.

At best, the poet is an anti-capitalist reciting passages from long dead, white men on economics, failing to think in new words or in new graphs or with new statistics about our current situation. He has forsaken structure for neat clichés, for lazy shibboleths, for self-congratulatory and hollow words of praise. His peers hold his hand, stroke his hair and paint signs for him decrying the apocalypse and neglecting the repetition of history and the hubris of his brethren who everywhere see burning buildings. But, these visions come only on account of the cocaine, MDMA, mushrooms that cloud his gaze, even if from long past days.

To the critic, suburbia is a wasteland, a battlefield, a corpse that has displaced birds and has failed to build Colosseums. If he longs to be part of a collective project himself, it is to a stillborn muse, to a school he wished he had founded or that finds new expression in an out-dated truth. He has failed to make up language itself and instead submits to camps and philosophies that are dusty and worn, to all kinds of projects that shun the sweat-inducing labour of unpacking where we stand today, on the always flowing lava that once was black sand. The critic, always seeking to be the fly in the ointment, is drowning in unreality. He is no canary in the coalmine, but a fear-mongering fancier, a falconer who eats a unique rat of tofurkey on the holidays, whose obscurity is built on the pyramid scheme of his relevancy.

But what has he done? What is the role of this critic for us now?

He is there to show the falseness of false false consciousness, a third order fakery that believes itself to have a kind of confidence because it knows how to doubt the bourgeoisie that we call suburbanite. But he does not know how the masses live; he does not toil in factories that make its commodities. He wrings his hands and feels guilty over the goods he craves, thinking that this awareness is enough for him to be better than the unthinking people who are his neighbours, who live in their ticky tacky tract homes with their knicky knacky tourist tchotchkes. But this critic is himself a peddler of mischief, a wanton and blatant illywhacker, a trickster, a hustler, a snake oil charmer who thinks he speaks a different language. He simply moulds word sculptures from the same shit the suburbanite works with each and every day. Where some say renovations, he says decoration. Where some complain about mortgages, he complains about wages. Where some suggest tax and spend, he offers his hand empty as it is, thinking that grants need to go up, and never thinking of himself as a type of lobbyist for his own special interest. Where some say team sport, he says collectives. Where some say entertainment, he complains about attention deficits. Where some suggest movement, he proposes stasis, everywhere taking for granted what is the context he is working in, thinking himself to be eccentric or idiosyncratic or marginal to the mainstream tastes that everywhere seem to leer and crowd at him.

He, the critic, claims victim while threatening everywhere to sue, claims bullying when he condones harassment and subterfuge. But his knives are spoons, good only for eating ice cream and getting on with being footloose. This critic does not know how to wound because what he thinks is a curse is really only a diagnosis. That is why he seeks out other critics, for the critic places too much emphasis on language, thinking of every word painstakingly, mind-numbingly, obsessive compulsively, even though he neglects to attend to his craft like a master. In the rush to get it published, he wants to be seen in his coterie as a kind of fellow traveller to the revolutions that will not come regardless. The critic has no reality, not even an imagined reality that he can share beyond a small circle of sycophants who think they are martyrs. The critic dies for a cause but is only a horse that bolted towards the stables looking for a master when we all know that the self-driving car is the future. The critic has forgotten the dialectic, of how to come into consciousness with an awareness of who is the lord and who is the bondsman, regarding these philosophies as the province of Others. And so, the critic forgets that suburbia is a place of the now, forgets that poetry is to be found in the plaster cast swan on the front verge, the flowers in the backyard, the social relations that come from knowing thy neighbour. And so, the critic is at a loss about what to do when he sees that truth is to be found in the watering restrictions suggested by the council, thinking instead that the crocodile tears he cries will be enough to keep his lettuces alive through the hottest summer on record.

*

The critic is wrong (kind of).

*

I see in the suburbs, the dreams of the people, the hopes poured like foundation concrete into gnomes and swimming pools and pads for plumbing; in the choices of supermarket aisles, the genius of our generation, in the hundreds of salad dressings such exquisite lyricism that one cannot help but see the home as a love poem where island bench thoughts of heaven become real; in the cheese and olives served before soup, the welcome hospitality of the normal, everyday family, which one finds in this style of life, in its relief from hunger and pain and terror. One sees through what the suburbs seem to be for the critic; beyond, before, behind it there is a possibility, a hope not yet acted on, of utopia, solidarity, freedom. It is where we go for the longed for rest after the commute from the city or after coming in from the fields that are burnt to stubble, returning from the camp or the jail cell or the tin can that is the plane that brought us from the other side of the world where it is winter and the gods claim to dwell. It is where you watch the news of our universe and begin to map out how your voice can be heard and your vote can count at every level. All that is there, here in the suburbs, where we can pick a quandong from the bough, where you can stand before a food court, a cornucopia of kangaroo tartare, char kway teow, dumplings made from the song of someplace else. This is the hope that comes from being halfway there, laugh-way there, from being on a drive between an apartment and acreage.

In these suburbs, you can watch the migrating birds, listen to a Nobel lecture and play with your child. You can find contentment and nourishment rather than being simply relaxed and comfortable. In the brick veneer and the renovated specifications one can re-define a sonnet or break a line or rhyme in the pantone colour of the year and speak of how you reapply the second coating to match the new tiles. In choosing furniture, one comes to think of beauty as a whole and in so doing, you see the grace of the quotidian and invite guests to marvel at the carpet in the mezzanine level. That is there in the humble homes of the suburbs, from one side of the world to another, from banlieus to periurban fringes, from strip malls to freeways, from planned towns to reclaimed villages. There, in those suburbs, we begin to see our place in the world, to share in a dance that makes a fateful embrace of death itself, nurturing the world to life and how. It is the announced belief in the forgotten, the cast out, the misrepresented, the hounded, for in its aberrant simplicity, between cable news and lawn games, it has sought out absolute knowledge of the real. It sees its truth as a virtue of how one can turn toward, beyond and with justice to the huddled and the abused, and liberate us all from a prison into a DIY catalogue that you find in your letterbox down the road from a public school that your kids go to where they sing aloud 'Let us progress!' 'For a better world!' 'Freedom Now!'

In those suburbs, where they talk about the weather and talk about the weddings of their nephews and just gossip and chatter, let us see the poetry in the community newsletter, the election day bake sale, the milk delivered to the doorstep on the morning after. Those are my suburbs – a home for the truth with a hope for all in this world.

8

Birds of a Mirror

In poetry, a bird is not only a bird. They bring colour, life, and meaning. They connect with nodes of association and reference other poems. They are ecological as much as political, cultural, and social symbols, and things-in-themself.

In many poetic works, the bird is used to re-assert the pastoral in a suburban *tabula rasa* of ennui, boredom, soullessness, and, ultimately, death. Jean Kent's 'In the Hour of Silvered Mullet (Kilaben Bay, Lake Macquarie)' – is a four part reflection on life in the suburbs; 'the land of the bland, a stranger might sniff' but in Kent's hands a reflective space of nature, people, task, labour, holiday. To take only the first part, we read of the poet walking the quiet streets at sunset. She is drawn from her home by birds. In the opening stanza Kent writes:

> It was the *tink* of king parrots in the native frangipani –
> then the white sail-rip past my windows of cockatoos –
> sounds of the day on its final tack
> which spinnakered me out into this twilight.

Birds here propel the 'I' out of the house and into the street for an evening constitutional. They are lively and alive – they 'tink' and 'rip' compounding each other through their shared vowel. This contrasts with the suburb, even as they are constitutive of it. The suburbs, which 'accost' her at the beginning of her walk are seen as 'quarter acre *mausoleums,/*

bungalows mugged by the dinner hour.' Save for a P-plated car that 'erupts' with 'expletives' that 'fart then fade, strange as circus elephants' trapped hoots', the streets are quiet. People are inside eating while the poet walks 'this twilight trail'.

There are specific images – 'a Volvo, shiny as a buttered knife, rests beside/ its long loaf of house'; 'fibro weekenders/not dolled up (yet); new Taj Mahals, curtained with sheets' – but these aid her memory of 'inland towns of childhood'. The memory, the thought, is interrupted by currawongs crying *'Come home now! Come home now!'*. For Kent, the currawongs' voices are 'like sunlight on pewter water/dazzling away an entire suburb's saucepan lids – /just as the bitumen turns a corner and swoops me wrapped in everyone else's dinner, fragrant as bait,'. What then are we to make of the birds here? They offer not only life in the face of the dead, built environment (the mausoleum, the tomb of the Taj), or the inanimate (the buttered knife) but they also offer us a way for the poet to be led.

If a sailing vocabulary ('sail', 'tack', 'spinnakered') reminding one of journey, travel, movement draws her out of domesticity, an allusion to the kitchen ('saucepan lids') draws her back into the home. And so, birds have a way of knowing when to come and when to go. Nature understands the poet in some sense. We could deduce from this, especially when read alongside Kent's other poems in this volume, that there is a desire to regard animals as part of a 'group spirit', a sort of redemptive and knowledgeable way in the world that informs the poet's memory and subject position. We are in the suburbs, but, dead as they are, we might prefer to be in the national park, the field, the ocean.

In 'In the Hour of Silvered Mullet', birds are the pastoral trope that tells us there is life inside the catacomb that is suburbia. We see something similar, namely that the suburb is dead and the bird is active, moving, alive, in Jamie Grant's 'Yacht Harbour – Stillness' ('silence embalms/ the suburbs'); S.K. Kelen's 'Saturn' ('suburbs died of fright'); Robert Adamson's 'Drawn With Light' ('suburbs of living dead'); Tim Thorne's 'Advice' ('waste', 'sick', 'cancer'); Henry Lawson's 'Interlude. Next Door' ('a suburb that hasn't the soul of a louse'); Dorothy Porter's 'Gossip' ('death/

is a boring smell/in a room/in a suburb'); Alan Gould's 'Kosciusko Essay' ('downward,/deathward'); David Rowbotham's 'The Birds of Berkeley' ('the suburbs of stoned Stephens'); and Ouyang Yu's 'Sex Notice' ('your suburb is too dead').

In contrast to this pastoral heraldry, a suburbanite rendering of birds is seen when they are presented as a form of ornamentation within the poem. They are there to add colour, to decorate without recourse to the fact that they are there to be life-giving amidst the deadness of the whole; that is to say they are 'featurist' in Robin Boyd's words. This is clearly demonstrated in 'O, Kingfisher' by Dorothy Porter. In this poem, Porter is aware that the bird is 'exotic', but the reader also apprehends the word 'azure', which, in the plain speech of the rest of the poem, seems exceptional if not defamiliarising. 'Fatigued' works with 'resigned' and 'guise' – they are words apart but together in their apartness. 'Azure' may correlate with 'jungle' because of the sound, but both only compound azure's separateness. It is the striking, featurist word of the poem.

We also get a featurist word amid plain speech to describe birds in Gig Ryan's 'Past' ('plangent') and Thomas W. Shapcott's 'In the Town' ('melisma'). These are the words one may need a dictionary to explain. In Porter's 'Scenes from A Marriage I' the suburb itself becomes 'swish', 'dangerous', 'glamorous', 'gamey', 'golden', 'exhilarating' *because* of a bird. In this poem, the night parrot, a symbol of nature and mystery, perhaps extinct, brings the suburb into a sort of modernist, urban, dangerous realm. When the night parrot is considered as a counterpoint to Kirchner – a German expressionist painter whose work was considered degenerate under the Nazis and who committed suicide in 1938 – and El Dorado – a mythic American city of gold – we have a complex interaction between country and city, nature and human. The suburb though is a flashy thing because of the parrot. In this poem, if the parrot was not driving the car – symbol of the post-war suburban – one may assume we would not think either of Kirchner or El Dorado. This is a question of the suburb as a consuming, sprawling entity that builds on the featurism that Porter presents elsewhere.

A suburbanist rendering of birds is demonstrated when there is ambiguity to the interpretation, which is to say that the suburb is not dead and that the bird is not there as an antithesis rendered as life. In other words, birds are part of the suburbs. As Robin Boyd writes, 'forms and spaces can be a delight in themselves without an observer feeling any needs for features.' Nowhere is this clearer than Geoff Page's 'The Birds'. In that poem, the speaker 'flaps up to join them'. It is a suburb that is run by birds ('an aviary about the house'). He does 'glide off over the suburbs', but we can reflect on whether he will return with these birds. We are unsure whether the person wants to identify with the birds as an *escape* from the suburbs or whether he simply wants to engage with being *about the house*. In either case it collapses his humanimality into the Othered position – he becomes them, able to escape. It is not so much about remaining a suburbanite then, but escaping from it in such a way that he allows himself to get deeper into the structure. It is, after all, 'their' home.

This suburbanist ambiguity of separation from and connection to is also evident in Adamson's 'Drum of fire' ('In the park/I flew with rainbow lorikeets/and hung upside down in the branches of flowering coral trees') and Julian Croft's 'Suburbs' ('the boyfriend hurtles past bird-bodied'). There is also a sense in the following poems that the birds are an integral part of a suburb that is *living*: Philip Salom's 'Planes' (stanza one); S.K. Kelen's 'Creatures'; Rowbotham's 'Coorparoo' ('the cottages are cotes'); Jill Jones' 'April's Rescue' ('the second nesting since we've lived here'; 'we adopt their nurturing'); Adam Aitken's 'The Reply' ('like the silence between trees/ filling slowly with the songs of birds/ you could transcribe as the happiness/of the woman my speech could never keep'); Douglas Stewart's 'The Dreaming World' (stanza two); Pam Brown's 'Seven Days' ('Home' to 'installed for them'); Vivian Smith's 'Early Arrival: Sydney' (stanza one); Katherine Gallagher's 'Entente' (stanza one); Murray's 'Equanimity' ('More natural to look at the birds about the street, their life/that is greedy, pinched, courageous and prudential/as any of these bricked tree mingled miles of settlement'; 'bird minds and ours are so pointedly visual').

Birds are found everywhere in poetry, but they often are able to be the lens through which we can see the pastoral, the suburbanite, the suburbanist in such a way that we understand the qualities of poems, that we can organise our thoughts as though they have wings rather than being caged by the world itself.

9

Notes of a Malayali

I first went to my ancestral village in Kerala in 1994. After short periods there, I returned for an extended stay in 2016–2017. This period also included the demonetisation of the economy on 8 November 2016, which was a remarkable moment in history that impacted on the daily life of people in countless ways. I mentioned it in the earlier chapter 'Big Box Island'. It ran alongside the colonial and seemed to me to be an instance of a new soft-structuralism. In any case, Kerala is a polytheistic place with roots that predate the Portuguese then Dutch then English colonisation. According to myth, Kerala rose up from the water when Parasurama threw his axe into the water and the land rose up to return it to him. Since then, Kerala has also created forms of governance, culture and religion that responded to these world historical systems, which helps one read poets with nationally Othered origins who live on this continent now. To my mind, it is not only that it is a post-colonial polity, but that the enduring quality of the place is rooted in pre-colonial, para-colonial, decolonised realities as people live them out. That matters for thinking through other places, and this essay comes out of that milieu with specific points of reference about diasporic Asian subjectivity more generally.

For many poets, the question of decolonisation is figured to be a question of land. Many tend to mean land in the way that it approximates nature, which is to say land resembles undeveloped frontier, is located in the Western Pilbara rather than Western Sydney. Many complement this with discussion of cities and suburbs, too, but it is land many are speaking of first and foremost.

Yet, if we know that conversations of decolonisation are not intended to be conversations simply situated 'out there' and if we know that this is a task for the contemporary citizen no matter where they live, what does a post-settlement poetics look like now? It might mean re-interpreting the continent in a basic sense; it might mean apprehending the social life that is here at the moment and asking what is another truth that sits adjacent to what we already know. Part of that means thinking of the work of poets of colour who come from other colonies. It means thinking of colonisation as a world historical system that is beyond the national; one that sees a family resemblance between India, South Africa, the Caribbean, as well as the resistance to it. In that, it is not about finding a perfect position from which to speak. If you are sitting on stage, you are taking up space. If you are telling us we need to hear from the silenced, we are already listening to your truth. If you are there to suggest you are a voice of the Other, beyond reproach and privilege, you have forsaken the retrospection needed to push the discourse into the future because of the shifting realities of power in our times. What that means, is that those who speak for the subaltern are already within us, and, if we are to look at the foundation, if we are to look at the base beyond liberalism's identity politics, we need to look to a new understanding of what it is to be a victim of empire in the networks that we belong to. That is what it might be to decolonise no matter what diaspora we are from.

Next to this acknowledgement of place and power is the sheer fact of suburbia's materiality when it comes to an emergent world historical system. Suburbia is where a lot of people live and is an existential, material, and spiritual common ground. In that way decolonisation, post-colonisation, uncolonising intersects with suburbia in its potential, including convincing an unwilling hegemony of transformation and the liberation that comes from systems of power that are inherited, projected, forced onto everyday citizens. Hegemony in settler societies and elsewhere surely means people who live in the suburbs most of all and not simply a white majority. The private property dream might be harder to come by, but it is still the hope of the Average Joe, regardless if that is the Average Habib, Average

Moorumburri, or Average Josephine. So, what are we to make of one particular poetic expression that speaks of its diasporic identity with a suburban consciousness that somehow contributes to uncolonising us?

I turn here to Omar Sakr's *These Wild Houses*. Judith Beveridge states in her introduction to the book that the poems:

> … take us to the core of what he has experienced as a 'queer Muslim Arab Australian from Western Sydney, from a broke and broken family.'

However, it also seems fruitful to read *These Wild Houses* through the lens of suburbia as well, especially as a way of defining a condition of being in the world that we are blind to while also being materially saturated in. Poetics can bring to consciousness what is immediately around it, and, as Martin Duwell stated when writing of 'Sestet Number 5' in Lachlan Brown's *Limited Cities:*

> … you do get the sense that the distinctive life of the suburb, if entered into fully, can generate a distinctive kind of poem, attuned to unusual but telling elements.

In other words, the poem becomes a way to generate an intentionalised understanding of suburbia, which involves renewing belonging.

Sakr's suburbia is a complex place, not altogether bewildering but filled with precariousness, violence, and haunting. In a recurrent motif, grass is always described as 'blades'. Consider for example 'Botany Bay', which reads:

> On a grassy plain overlooking Botany bay
> two men pray, facing the East
> kneeling to sea. Children windmill
> around the spit of land, squinting
> in the heat as seagulls, bellies puffed

and ready to fight for scraps, tear
at each slim gift.
Blankets anchor double dates
on the green, the pebbled cliffs and sand.
Fish and chips steam in sun.
A couple walks with banh mi
in hand. Before me is spread pide, eggs,
cucumber and focaccia. Over there, my aunty
says, is Captain Cook's museum.
Through the haze, it looks both close
and awful in its distance, a thin bridge
connecting it to us. My grandmother,
too worn by salt and earth and time
for the rigours of prayer, just sits
rocking, faith on her split lips and skin.
Imagining the invasion, I lie upon blades
of grass, staring up at the hijabbed sky
footprinted with clouds and wonder
what Cook would have made of this.

There is, of course, a tradition of Captain Cook poems from Henry Kendall and Barron Field to Kenneth Slessor to A.D. Hope. But what I want to draw attention to is the historicising in this poem, which involves the juxtaposition between the quotidian symbols of our present including the celebrated 'diverse' foods next to an image of the explorer as an archetype of invasion. Everything is saturated with the knowledge that this is stolen land and everyone is trying to find a way to belong, even the new migrant.

Yet, it might be less about reifying particular sides and more about asking what comes next? To ask that is to ask: how can we belong to tomorrow? One answer to that lies in the hope of the suburbs. This runs alongside the question of decolonisation in our own time and it is a question of para-colonial routing that matters here now. This is a style of life that Sakr begins to depict even if that is often through negation and absence.

Read in this way, his poem 'What the Landlord Owns' becomes less a self-contained image of the domestic and more a political metaphor. At the end, it states:

> … I sit at my desk
> breathing deep the pungent spices of their dinner,
> the cold scent of their arguments while shadows
> clothe the hallway of my home and I see
> that hunger precipitates movement. Steep
> stairs make descent dangerous, I take them at a run
> when I can no longer stand empty. The dining
> table is covered in books, old and new,
> the words of dead men and women gathering
> dust, their resurrection in me a matter of wait.
> The oven can only be lit with a tapering flame
> coupled with a prayer, the fridge so old it sing-speaks
> Langston and the go-go washing machine
> has the laughter of a tap dancer trapped
> inside it flits with every task it is set. Two minutes on
> is all it takes to heat up a meal before I return
> to my window, desk and the strait of stars
> guiding surf in the dark above these families
> living near, unaware the house and light on the hill
> are ruptured within, choking with three separate ways
> of silence.

This close up focus allows us to imagine what a public space that radiated out from such a hearth may be. In its remorseless critical eye and muted hopes, it gives a new sheen to 'mateship'. This could be the solidarity of silence that happens in a house, which is the 'light on the hill'. This is a message from the margins. Sakr's world is a world that is diverse, a world of different characters held together by common experience, understandable plain speech, and a coherent subjectivity. In this poem, it is books and domestic goods that do this work of suturing 'us' together, wounded as 'we' are. This does not, inter alia, mean that *These Wild Houses* is liberal or lyrical or not post-modern, rather that it comes at a different moment, which requires us to challenge the very assumptions of our colonially Othered poetics. One way into thinking of that is to ask what colonisation was, and how it sits next to other discourses saturated with power, in their family resemblance to each other as systems of world historical importance.

In that, one would assume that the title of Sakr's book – *These Wild Houses* – refers to houses that are wild. But 'houses' is not only a noun. It is also a verb meaning 'to accommodate', to contain, store, hold, retain. 'Houses' is a homonym and although it would be more correct to say 'these wilds house' or 'this wild houses', one could speculate that in their current expression the wild houses do indeed host school fetes, charity auctions, cake stalls, having included kebabs and halal snack packs along the way. This is not land, or an ecopoetics, in the common axis, but the wild as an ideal, an ideal that Sakr avoids precisely because his suburb is constantly threatening and threatened.

Poetry of this kind can work as a way to raise consciousness and in so doing act as a bulwark against the selective caricature of 'authenticity', which commercial publishers would seem to demand in a simple expression of 'market taste'. In other words, this is not a hate race that finds nothing redemptive in suburbia. But, the onus on us is to see its raw materiality and not its obvious negations. It understands, in a complicated way, in a way that is self-aware, what it means to be where we all stand, to uncover this, to rename and express it, is the task of the reader. Sakr's wilds of suburbia are one place that might help us move beyond the congealed debates of empire and towards an idea of place that is not merely unsettled, but is an ideal possibility that knows its reality in the world. For many, the aspirational expectation is for a suburban style of life, but it is up to us to demonstrate that this is compatible with a form of republican sovereignty that responds to calls for recognition, treaty, the republic, a bill of rights, and land restoration. That is the task before us as poets and as citizens as well.

In thinking about forms of ideology and poetic authorship, I want to think through Lachlan Brown's *Lunar Inheritance* next to, after, with Omar Sakr. Brown's is a work about consumption, food, language, family and identity. It too is a diasporic poetics that speaks back to nation from a position that is outside it in part. As an imagined community, there are a number of ways to discursively construct this place, which is variously glossed as a colony, a settler society, stolen land, a free state and, even, as politicians would have it 'the most successful multicultural nation in the world'. Yet our raced complicatedness upsets the neatness of this last myth, something addressed in Brown's 'Filling out a Form', which states:

> Classed
> as mashed-potato-fried-rice-vigour-half-caste
> you won't symbolise the best of what
> the country's categories allow (not
> that you care).

That poem is partly about the opposition to belonging that diverse people feel here, our daily experiences that would upset the boosters of our tolerance, equality, and acceptance.

Thinking about *Lunar Inheritance* means thinking about what a diasporic poetics opens up. How can we come more fully into a national self-consciousness given our suburbanity? And, how is that different from the discourses around settlement, colonisation, race? What can diaspora teach us about the future we might come to inhabit in this land here and now?

Gaetano Rando writes in 'Negotiating the Liminal Divide':

> Diasporic poetics is, arguably, also very much a poetics of engagement with the liminal divide, a process that is not linear but cyclic, as crossings in liminal space and time join an implicit, complex and not altogether unproblematic but

> nevertheless positive present to recall the joys and sorrows of an ever-present pre-migration past.

For Rando, the relationship to history in a diasporic poetics is about repeating waves that shift and change but are nevertheless inventions towards a future that 'we' can be proud of. It is not a simple nostalgia predicated on romanticising where one 'comes from' nor is it about alienation and fragmentation in a new place. Rather, it is a relationship that means one can inhabit two places, that one chews gum and walks at the same time, feeds dogs as well as swine. We might add to Rando and suggest that this liminality is central for a number of imagined communities. *Lunar Inheritance* is a work that engages with this because it comes out of homelands new and old. It enters into a condition of diasporic thinking and extends Brown's first book *Limited Cities*. That first work was firmly grounded in Brown's home suburb of Macquarie Fields. When one reads *Lunar Inheritance* with *Limited Cities* in mind, one knows that Brown is going somewhere else, somewhere away from the suburbs of Bruce Dawe. Brown's shift is not, I would speculate, for the reasons Geoff Page reads into his debut, namely that:

> The suburbs don't have the prefix 'sub' in them for nothing. In Brown's case it is the 'limited' suburbs of southwest Sydney, with their somewhat depressed populations (albeit aspirational in parts) to whom Brown (almost like a Whitman) quietly offers himself as poet. It's hardly an art of celebration, however – but nor is it one of disdain. It's more the feeling that life doesn't need to be this bad but also that there's no simple way out … This inaugural collection deserves a wide readership, even if its truthfulness is quite often depressing. Paradoxically, however, the artistry of Brown's observations tends to uplift even as what he portrays fills us with melancholy, if not shame.

Page's irreconcilable confusion (depressed/aspirational; celebration/disdain, uplift/melancholy) only suggests that his reading of *Limited Cities* lacks generosity towards the content as well as an understanding of the type of life that is possible in suburbia itself. *Limited Cities* apprehends the centrality of the suburbs with insight and care to suggest an engaged remove. It knows that to have a suburban consciousness is, in some sense, to be a hybrid of the city and the country as well as their best attributes, to be a 'half-caste' of places somewhere between downtown and outback. As Brown writes in his poem 'Macquarie Fields. Autumn's edge 2005', 'I am somewhere in between I think.' That he is 'near this part/of the city that is not/the city' means he is articulating what it is to be suburban and how to respond to urbanity, and with it, one expects modernism and its discontents.

This diasporic liminality is central to *Lunar Inheritance.* It is the work of a hybrid, this time on the axis of ethnicity. The content would still be part of the field whose aim is to 'know thyself', which is not quite the same as being a poetry of self-expression. And so, we could re-read Brown less as a bard of suburbia and more as a poet thinking through his immediate surrounds including the closest of subjects – family. This means there is a more philosophical shade, if not an ecumenical breadth and beatific openness to his oeuvre as a whole, which invites the reader to turn to a genealogical history, a journey into the self as it develops an awareness of what it is as it travels to and from 'home', into a diasporic poetics as critique of simple nation as well. And so, if Brown has lost his place, or found another after Macquarie Fields, he has not lost his Way at all.

The best way to see Brown's Way is through paying careful attention to the suburban concerns of consumerism, food and language. One knows that Brown's identity, or the identity of the poet speaking, is found in these expressions again and again. These are the important ways of how he relates to the world. In terms of consumption, there is the acknowledgement that 'it's all made in China, made in China, made in …' Brown not only sees the conspicuous purchases of the rich (a Mercedes in Shanghai) but also those of the everyday people who roam the malls and convenience stores of an expanding post capitalist-communist world. This focus on consumption ties in with hoarding in Brown's own family but it feels neither judgmental nor apolitical, precisely because the poet is also complicit. This is simply the world he lives in even if we do not like it. As he writes in '(making a man)':

> You try to remix every belt in the belt shop
> then, suit suit suit, tie tie tie, plastic wrapping
> you can dispose of yourself, along with that
> jacket you bought just to have a chance of fit-
> ing in. But size means nothing here, a history
> presses into your shoulders, and the young
> assistant's hands reach around your throat
> tightening sale time love overstock delight.

It is not only the market though that has its hands around your neck. For Brown, it is also there in the people who Other you, seen in various explorations of racist abuse that target the poet and his family. As he writes in '(life-hyphen)':

> The way you don't know (what) you are in Austral-
> ia until someone yells out 'Fucken gook' from the
> bus window is the way you don't notice the Guang-
> zhou rain falling until you look up and it has slick-
> ed over everything and you find your skin wet and
> trembling but the light's polished grey modulations
> mean people stop double-taking at your distortion-
> pedal face just long enough for you to get past them.

The combining of abuse with rain is a compressed juxtaposition of something hateful with something potentially beautiful. It forces us, like the people in the poem, to double take while the poet himself moves on. This idea of language as pointed, demonstrated here by the act of verbal abuse, recurs in the volume and it is not always negative. Sometimes it allows Brown to assimilate into the nation in a way that helps with mitigating or pre-empting or stopping abuse. Language often comes as a buttress, support, pleasure and the volume does delight in common poetic techniques like repetition, rhyme and rhythm even as Brown is aware of their limits. As he writes in '(afterimage when you can't look directly at the sun)':

> And language is already straining this experience
> like a half-hearted net in a swiftly flowing river,
> catching the large stuff, bringing it fresh
> to the table, but letting too much slide by.

But, what does this accumulate into? Thinking about consumerism, language and food come together in the poem '(distant sister)', which states:

> The murmur of shoppers becomes a river that has long disappeared
> and we are both silently reading poems as the food grows cold
> and I imagine our mothers telling us that we must now eat
> and in one afternoon this city of dust has become like a
> flame held too close to my skin and I feel it peeling me back
> exposing my heartbeat like a huge mechanical sea turtle.
> And later, when you quietly begin to sing, the streets stretch out
> along mythic meridians and suddenly I'm afraid to walk them alone.

This poem is, of course, one of vulnerability, but it is also full of image and metaphor – the shoppers being a natural force, the city of dust, the heartbeat a mechanical turtle. This coupling of urban and country images suggests that there is a space between the two, a kind of hybridity that is a synthesis, being suburban all at once. And to articulate that, to simply call it into existence, is to suggest that one is precarious. Even with song, the 'I' is afraid to walk alone in the myths that have boxed us in, the myths that might be explained as the congealed ones of streets where abuse is hurled at your brother and mother or in the Hurstville BBQ restaurant where your dad is the only white guy in the place even if his fork joyously 'divides joints and marrow, tendons and tripe'. And this dislocation, this quivering, this questioning is there too when you arrive in your ancestral country and you write in '(some introduction required)':

> You step off the plane in Shanghai
> and vomit into your sleeve which
> is no way to greet the past or future,
> with time running on like that stream of passengers
> passing your inert body, now keeled over
> in the airbridge. And then, when your wheeled
> suitcase somehow carried you down Nanjing Rd
> like a hospital gurney, you find the city's voice inside your own.

The entry is a difficult one, one that the body feels and rejects, that is an ignored spectacle made explicitly into a disease or injury or emergency. As a poet, you have taken on something you had to but did not quite know how. Yet the failure to perfect the speaking, the failure of being a poet who can be diasporic, suburban, authentic is about the structural condition in which the poetry is read. One still needs a suit after all, even if one knows the shopping assistant's hands are around your neck as is the government and every racist citizen in your 'home' nation.

The failure of return though, of coming to Shanghai and vomiting, or of broadening the accent in country pubs, is about the failure of 'authenticity'. In other words, the expectation of wholeness and welcome, which will wash away the existential anxiety of being Othered, abused and ostracised in the new place falls short. 'China' will never be home because it is always changing, and home is never as simple as we have been led to believe, not least of all in the nation with its legacy of colonisation as Sakr paints it and the ongoing white privilege that is unconscious in most critics. We cannot return to something we never quite apprehended anyway, and so, I am reminded of Shen's lines that went 'I am so tired of writing about/

being Chinese as if it were/ a loss'. Hope is there in family, in relations, in heritage, in religion, in poetry itself.

Lunar Inheritance is not the simple rediscovery of roots, of coming to know oneself as part of 'a people', even as such a reading would conveniently impose an imaginary coherence on the experience of dispersal and fragmentation. Nor is it a simple commentary on being abused as a diasporic minority. Instead, the poems are often mutable, ongoing, processive, contextual and becoming, and this allows us to refuse a simple understanding that it is merely about loss. This is not about the loss of identity, but the aging of oneself as a family member, about the lament that happens with the passing of time and the nostalgia that all this implies. This expression of identity is historical then, meant here as part of a materialist conception of the world that looks back on itself in such a way that aspires to balance. This is not sentimental or saccharine or weepy, but reserved and observant. It is a close-in book, a work of intimacy that is nevertheless part of structures that exist in the world including race and racism. It is through an intimate identity though that we begin to think of our own peculiar and particular travels, where we relate as individuals and ask ourselves as readers – how do I know where I come from and where I go? The answer to that, at least for Brown, might be found in Macquarie Fields, back in the suburbs we thought we left behind, and the future that it brings with it, alongside Sakr's own imperative to locate a home in the wildness of the world itself.

10

Theory Ordinaire

The banal expression of occupation in settler societies today is the suburbs. This is the case in Argentina, Brazil, New Zealand, Siberia, the United States, and Canada. This is not to suggest that we do not see cases of direct violence or that there are not sovereign peoples in them or that suburbs do not exist in other nations or that the suburbs do not border the city or country. It is that we fail to think through the collective material and ideal life in them in a language game that is from them. In other words, we lack autonomous translations of this critique that are immanent to this style of life. We have yet to dissemble them. Since their development as an object domain of distinction in the post-World War Two era, precious little has been written about the material culture, intangible heritage, and quotidian expressions in such a way that it accumulates into a congealed historical understanding. Now that the Anthropocene is discussed in contemporary discourse, it seems that the owl that flew at dusk has made it through till dawn and we can see our era in a new light prior to its fading once more. In other words, we can cognise what suburbanism is precisely because it continues to exist and is passing.

Suburbanism is the retrofitting of the suburbanite that recaptures the original utopian *Geist*. The poetic expressions of anomie, alienation, straightjacketing, morbidity, and shame that convey a suburbanite sensibility need to be challenged by close reading the archive, which displays the infinity of experience. We need to find the positive emotional entrainments as expressed in linguistic rituals. This can be used to undermine a '68 generation that has created a historical consciousness that Oedipally holds onto an anti-sentimental yet falsely nostalgic 1950s. This is their death drive that simply relocated narcissism into itsself by denying the pleasures and good life of its parents. Rebellion never seemed so conceited, conquered or derivative. That the 1960s are held onto as a revolutionary moment only suggests the way in which they were conservative at heart, precisely because their performative affect was countered by a failure to attend to the spirit, politics, and history of structures. The reification of rights precisely when power had shifted from juridical-legal settings to corporations is simply one example of the strategic failure of 'the Left' at this time.

The perceived uneven distribution of futurity and resources that allows claims of avant-gardism to persist has resulted in a belief that ideas will one day percolate, that language was the ladder by which we climbed into tanks and planes and trains. The reasons people do things are much more complex. Every manifesto need be interpreted, translated, misapplied, contested, and re-written. How that is done will surely depend on the context of intelligibility one carries in one's body, which is the liberation of the soul, as much as the space one enters into, and the sources from which one grows. If the author is dead, the reader is alive; if the work is undefined, the society knows why.

That we need to create terms and phrases that decalcify historically leaden ones speaks to the freedom of anti-collusive thought. The unpacking of this depends on how one is able to negotiate the positioning that comes from conservative theorists, particularly from the self-congratulatory liberalism that initially appears progressive. No one has greater recourse than to consider how commoditised they are – one's ethics need be judged by how one buys, spends, acts if one wants to think through one's base assumptions. Hence, the necessary reclamation of suburbia, which is unsustainable, rationalised, bloated, consumptive, and aspirational. Resistance starts here because this belt decides where power lies by its ballot, by its dollar, and by its soft projective power, which manifests in cultural tastes transmitted worldwide. This means our activism of the possible needs to acknowledge that this is a nerve centre for our present life. It is not simply that we must stop climate change through anti-capitalist enterprise, which seems boneheaded given the polluting possibility in communist countries. It is that to live good lives we must be in service to an ecologically minded, which is to say worldly, sign system of living and engagement.

Poetics is a specific and special field consisting of poems, their connective tissue, and *mabarn*. A poem is a language puzzle within that, and, when read dialectically, it can be a sacred or profane act dependent on the reader whose frame is determined by their emotional entrainment through status groups' micro-interactive ritual chains. How we examine poetry depends in part on the linguistic sources that determine our frame, what we deem to be possible, and the capital we wish to accrue in that setting. That means any linguistic artefact can contain a poetics, where a linguistic artefact is understood semiotically as a symptomatic focal point for the network. The 'classics of world literature' then are simply those with a perceived density that has accumulated through translations into recognisable rituals if not contested truth content. And so, legislation is the forgotten poetry of history. But, it demands attention as an artefact of language to be close read precisely because of its implication. We could mean that, for poets, the Constitution is something worthy of as much interrogation as Seamus Heaney's 'Lightenings' or Derek Walcott's 'The Bounty'. This is about the application of frame to the raw material at hand. That this would be original only misconstrues the argument that needs rebuttal, namely that repetition is not inter alia negative capital. Our fetish for the reboot simply because it appears new does not warrant its immediate validation.

What constitutes something new relies on a perceived absence in the archive. But, the archive is infinite; the regression is infinite. That is to say, we can talk and talk about nothing at all till the cows come home whether that nothing is 'time' or 'being' or 'mind' or even just plain old 'nothing'. My work challenges the dictum that we need 'make it new' or return to the Greeks for answers or that ideas do not matter. Through language as that social and tangible thing we participate and change the world, which surely does exist. This is not through the unoriginality of genius but through the presence of history today as a proliferative resource that offers only more questions. This is as much about answering 'what is a poem?' in a positive sense as it is about suggesting that the conditions in which we ask such a questions need unpacking as surely as any specific language. Part of that condition is undeleting our sensibility as readers through challenging the acceptable boundaries of authorial insertion. I make that statement as a white man and a brown one who is validated by their supposed heightened experience, which serves only to render and anthropologise my philosophical discourse as something beyond my own. My first hand is still my right hand is still my write hand. Empire's challenges exist insofar as we live discursively inside them. Our negation perpetuates it, while our ignorance de-blisses it.

Suburbanism as a re-organisation of thought enables us to re-negotiate the terms of trade precisely because it is emergent and rich. It offers us a way to critique any such polity that is predetermined to be suburban, and not simply as a new intellectual commodity that can be assimilated, reified and fetishised by an unresponsive and unchanged structure. It is not about raw material being value added by critical scholarship but about undoing the academy from a located perspective that is not not nomadic. In this, one not only means the nation, the geography, the landmass, but also the systems of thought, the ideas, the language, all of which are porous albeit gripped by the 'space' of a transnationalism, global Anglophonia and world studies.

That theory is thought to be the province of Europe, without an adequate provincialising of the said continent, and America dominating the contemporary scholarly field means we see that peripheries provide ore, wheat, fleece. This is only a useful heuristic that needs challenging, which can be done by reversal. This overturns the false consciousness that unduly siloes the possible by reinforcing the limits of History. A revolution is necessary and it must come from the suburbs. That it has already happened may be the case for the dead, even as reclaiming their joy remains one possible dialogic unobligation that allows us to see through to a saner world. Thus, it is not about deconstruction of today through past action, but the re-participation in and reconstruction of presentism in order to enable a precise vulgarity. That my morning shit can become fodder for the tree that becomes the paper in this book is the absolute point. It should not be flushed out to sea, which is not to suggest that science knows what is what on a grand scale or that I have ceded ground to its expertise on the basis of enlightenment faith alone, especially because sovereign traditional knowledge systems approach the most complex hydro geographies. It is that I prefer not to swim with toxins, which might be because it is in dangerous poor taste that destroys my gut flora and ruins my skin. What is necessary is the permaculturisation of poetics, considered here to be a question for philosophy, history, politics, economics, which are simply disciplinary ideal types worthy of interrogation, creative destruction and renewal.

Aesthetics as the apprehension of the surface of things is precisely where the depth of available light lies. Suburban expressions of that need be attended to by aesthetic consideration. The suburbanite rendering might be fast food involving agribusiness modes of production; might be pornography involving meat market modes of production; might be elite academies involving publish or perish modes of production; all of which rest on casualised pools of labour that refute the long term through a paradoxical and affective performative obsession with liveliness now; all of which share a certain exploitative tendency that nevertheless feels good even as one can puncture the gloss by asking what happens after my death, which is to say a symbolic end. The moral righteousness of the neo-hippy capitalist would have us believe in organics, tantra, and mindfulness failing to see how their structural approximation is its own industry that need be questioned. This is not to disagree with the market, but to ask what is the market to begin with? Where are our suburban rituals? What happens in the food court, passionate marriage and intellectualising publics?

Historicising the foundations means we can ruin buildings and build ruins, which might be the best possible outcome when we live on shifting sands and bleached coral bandwidth. We could go elsewhere, to firmer ground on othered islands or yet more fluid oceans free from microplastics if not lava eruptions. There are genealogical networks to be made that point us towards the direction we need to go in, that start to map out a way where we do not have to find our way about. I am speaking here of the poetics of suburbanism, be that the pink trim of an Iced Vovo in the supermarket aisle that captures the attention of the shopper in such a way that they think of eating it with tea rather than focus on the two layers of plastic wrapping.

You might say 'I like what I like' but everyone is beset by trying to know thyself and live a good life, which is to say, we all try come to terms with what the 'I' is and what it likes. I like to eat octopus or so I tell myself due to the memory of what tastes 'nice'. I also want to be good, so need to have balance, and to balance the knowledge of its sentience with the belief that it is a relatively sustainable food given the acidification of oceans worldwide. We cannot only eat bread and drink water, even as we enjoy certain types of them when we do and we should be thankful that we are not thirsty no matter what that means or where we are situated. But nor should it stop us from wanting more where we appear to know what 'want' is and 'more' is too. That is a fundamental right whose origins need not be obscured by the suggested contours of an inalienable total system, even as we see totality in opposition especially. All things are not alike; all things are not similar. Every life is unique though the bounds of where one starts and one begins is indeterminate – breast milk provides antibodies; bones provide lime for worms.

In the study of poetics, one could imagine a study that placed verse from anytime next to verse from anyplace, and together this assemblage would become unitary, if not singular, through an interpretive voice. We create, enact, enable a status group when we speak of it. This is not simply to highlight performative utterances, but to suggest that the very structure of language itself is real and has a function when applied to cultures of honour. In other words, idealists find greater succour in language (narrowly defined) than materialists, even as the latter trade, barter, speak, converse in money, itself a phantasm. The gift that is the unpaid-for reading, the 'free' entertainment being a spoken engagement of poetry, is distinct from the coffee at a systemic level but not para-structurally. One still need exist in a market, but a market is only to be understood as a particularly rich metaphor; one could use 'game' or 'ritual' in another iteration. One could also use 'ecosystem'. But each word is contested, fought for, fraught, loved, rooted, freely radicalised and its own network. So is every other word. It leads us yet further still, yet deeper into the language as a whole, it is a box with endless 'hope' not thought of as a principle here but a living unfolding reality. That some words have an ostensible greater multiplicity of meanings only confirms that language is a minefield that shifts while simultaneously clusterfucking us all so well. Lexical conflict is evident in homonyms for example, which may open us out to musings on the continued relevance of hybridity or the paucity of double consciousness despite their continued deployment in ways that garner academic, and even cultural, capital. This is not to discount their validity but to suggest that we need a new set of keywords in order to reinvigorate the discipline in such a way that it eludes the machinations of big capital, if only because it is not us, and is responsive to the textual demands we place on criticism as if it were artificially separated from creativity.

And so, this space I am working in may be called the 'superbase'. The superbase is that between the superstructure and the base, which would be a structure between the ideological apparatus and the repressive apparatus. It is that which does not in the first instance have a pragmatic or material impact yet is not idealistic alone. It is what we are all really in. Planting trees is different from writing pamphlets about planting trees which is different again from administering either of those things, which is not to say they cannot be united in a single individual who functions as different in different spaces. That many now work in offices where the daily life of the paid enterprise is similar only suggests that this space is the superbase; that suburban life is preoccupied with being super basic.

The response to the superbase condition is involved in its own realisation – the coming into consciousness is through those who negotiate between both linguistically separable entities. This means recontextualisation rather than defamiliarisation, which is to say the accumulation of defamiliarisation so that the structure is changed. Rather than the defamiliarisation being confined to a singular text working against an assumed field of language protocol, recontextualisation re-orients the whole field itself. This is not the urinal as sculpture but the gallery as experience. Ear work enables it, whereby the fluidity of both is cognised as opportunity to reveal foundational assumptions about what is basic and what is superstructural. This means that activism is a work of non-non participation precisely because it is a self-negating, aware propulsive tendency. If this seems like dense clarity it is intended as such precisely because we have learned that Thought to be recognisable need come to us in such a manner. That is what the language market, which is a cousin of a language game, expects and the leveraging of language rituals into it can only resist commodification so much. This is where incubation and realisation become vital, as does the superbasic acknowledgement that all rituals are markets and all markets are rituals. Their perfect intersection is what is desirable as an aesthetico-ethical ideational praxis will encourage the living of good lives against the condition of bare life.

In thinking through the past expectations of what constitutes bare life one notices that the limits of the aspirational begin to be mapped out at various points in time – running water in the late nineteenth century, electricity shortly after. Although the therapeutic ethos in its modern form (sport, leisure, cinema) predates the 1950s explosion in suburbia, one notices an appreciable rise in inbuilt obsolescence and consumption in this era. This is the start of the suburbanite life – car, television, backyard, commute, ranch home. If contemporary settler societies have built on top of this, most noticeably in the contemporary obsession with digital technology, we also see its negation through the very same tools. This is not to deny the unevenness of distribution, that particular people in remote communities or reservations have Facebook and holes in their walls concurrently. The necessary historiographical action involves reinterpreting as much as uncovering, involves saying the 1950s were truly revolutionary in a way that provides succour for us now beyond the Beat bohemia. The merits of this revolution are debatable, but in labelling it thus, we may begin to redefine the contours of our own moment in such a way that we re-cognise the possibilities of world consciousness now.

After all, the post-war era is when we gain a celestial Other in the moon (first with radio waves (1946) then satellite images (1952) then popular televised pictures (1971)) and when there is the application of universal bureaucratic systems (World Bank, Universal Postal Union, United Nations). The paradox then is that the Cold War is precisely the moment when the world begins to imagine its wholeness. It is not the case of an end of history, but that in singularity we see duality if we read homonymically. The investment in sustaining the Cold War paradigm is not only about the continued binaries of thought, which extends to heteronormative gender dynamics and raced thinking at the very least, but is also suggestive of the present investments and fault lines that keep us enslaved to prior economic models that distance us from the present ecological reality. It is not that capitalism is alive and well as post-communists would have us believe, it is that no thought has yet arrived to undo the totality of assuming anything more than some specific keywords, which have power in particular circumstances. Suburbanism moves us towards that precisely because it is aesthetico-ethical and brings about the end of each not simply through desystematising thought itself but also finding sustenance in community, network, solidarity. This is a collective, untimed task with which we can engage the humanities without discounting the necessary engagements of its unnamed, spectral oppositional Other.

The language of theory is a toolbox, but you can't use all the tools at once (unless of course you have many hands and a complex machine rather than a hammer and a nail). The world is complex, and simple, according to the story we tell and because of that we need all hands on deck to manifest what needs to be a better life for all those involved.

There needs to be a better life because there is a war going on. There is always a war going on somewhere, a grand epic struggle that is quotidian as it is re-definable, often for the soul and the land itself. That the soul is expressed in common objects like the quarter acre block, the station wagon, the grass oval, means that a peace need be brokered by parties who participate, live in, dwell in the spaces of possibility they provide. I imagine it is the same too wherever we find new world literature. It is that the war for the soul that is not only invested in the people who are present today, which obscures the reality of the land-place-thing, it is also that the *mabarn* of the past custodians sits within us. Sixty thousand years matters for us right now then. I mean this as a past and future project. Suburbia is sovereign land. Traditional owners can be suburbanists too. But we always need interrogate what those things mean rather than assume we know what they are too. They are bounded categories that live here.

Rituals have boundaries too but only as a suggestion, which is to say the endogenous and exogenous forms of expression limit, expand, bleed into and enable rituals that are similar and different. Every repetition becomes original. Hence, suburbanism is a structural question not a local answer. Here is one locale, Wembley to Redgate to the Upper West Side and back again. All these people have moved back and forth and through the suburbs most of all, to America, New Zealand, Canada, to help us lead good lives for they live them too. But, we now must lead the way by saying no problem is intractable, no question too hard to ask, if not answer, for in asking it we begin to redefine the limits of what is possible and come to terms with the possibilities that matter. We do not have to move postcodes. We cannot sell off the family farm because we do not own one.

Suburbanism as the interpretive lens and the interpreting subject relies on realising the past as our focal point is updated constantly. It is not about history alone but the frames that cohere around our sensibilities. The end of communism is not the end of history but the end of the nation state as a reference economically, the discursive apparatus despite the ongoing political dramas of citizenship, refugees and legislative limits. It is not only that the body has a history, but that to know history takes a language of the body to interpret.

There is no vacancy in suburbanism. On balance it is everywhere. By which one can mean to say that through an absence of negativity one finds the dialectic of negation. In a language ritual of increasing attachment, especially through critique cognised as againstness, one can detach from petty petulance, which is not to say through intensely felt subjectivity one approaches neutral honesty if not objectivity, which one aspires to precisely because it enables one to occupy a possibility of change if not change itself. Possibility need be acted upon, ideal need be materialised, but it is its own type of freedom, which enables an expression through its non of utopianism (seen here with the freighted innocence of un-arrived paradise in minds' eye, collective). One man's theft is another person's liberation. One man's ignorance is another person's knowledge. But, we work together on what that is through definition, on what makes the good by led consensus. The suspension of antimonies is the suspension of antibodies. Responsibility is a privilege not a guilty betrayal of a misinterpreted past. England has no rights here but it senses it has privileges precisely because this appears to be written in English. What then is a language?

The suburbanist is always already listening to a new language as if that was a speaking. We are our stomachs growling – eat kangaroo or buffalo, maintain good gut flora. One is born with this as a type of becoming for becoming is the suburbanist and we talk with our tongues most of all. But, taste is distant from land through chemical processes not our own. The pervasive presence of the new technological apparatus which is itself a techne has meant the implication of cyborgia where unpredicted and expected, unconscious and planned, engagement with life from gestational to afterword. This matters for being kicked from the nest.

Home-less-nest does not mean the start of philosophy necessarily or its end. The key is to not always open the door presented. The difference that needs to be made is similar to what ails us all. That this is specific and problematised need not be repeated compulsively but one need acknowledge redefining the course. The course in general has a linguistic core, but this is to provide a structural equivalent in what came before even as the liquid dynamics of time mean we must begin to see fields of distinction as displacing when there is already lore.

One could turn to a variety of texts to discover, unpack, create the macro geography of suburbanism. In our time this might be reality television, fast food franchises or grand sporting spectacles. This would neglect the dense specificity and specific density that coheres in the single line of a poem (or legislation), a bar of music or any moment that can be endlessly and suggestibly made whole again and again. Shakespeare is an industry for a reason, so too garlic production, but we might not need to explain why in order to get closer to his aura. This is not to validate one form of critique or to worship translation over another or to merely point out what seems patently obvious with regard to importance. It is to suggest the contours of our questioning need persist for them to be more than this. A cat video tells us an awful lot but not as we know it. There is no need to start with the commodity but there is not not one. Something similar could be said of the letter, word, phrase, TV episode, Facebook post. In other words, entire systems can be built from single sell organisms. That is why suburbanism is an ecosystem. That the ecosystem appears to be in peril due to global warming means that the problem is one of incommensurability between timescales of political action and scientific thought, as if defining those two was possible at all, which is not to say we cannot do it all. The redistribution of goods where one acknowledges the apparent difficulty of defining both these things in service of a greater possibility is that in honey, wind or plastics. Animals appear on the peripheries of metropoles because of the lack of voting rights and their confinement to home contexts read here as natural but this neglects the domestic pet and the packaged flesh. That sex is metaphorised as this kingdom means even our intimate spaces (or public) are erogenised at a linguistic level in regards to something abased.

At some point in time many people pass through the suburbs even as that depends on the poles of reference, North-South, country-city, centre-periphery. One can be suburbanist without having lived in Seacaucus. They are not only in settler societies either but extend to modes of growth and decay in many countries and nation states. The becoming state may be found even when we're awake. Where one need be embraced is in the maintenance of endangered traditions whose importance is warranted if not through the accumulation of already acknowledged capital then through the necessary spiritual attachments that are of course material and allow us to promote an unwashed sustainability. Even that which melts started as solid. Even celebrities are workers, stars that fade, who appear to have owners. There is infinite progress that regresses into light. This holds for every thing, person, dream, word.

Every person is a performer but not all the world is a stage. Every one is damaged but the axis of that is dynamic. Everyone has baggage – get someone else to carry it with you or put it down yourself. The great men of history are compost for us all, even in this age. They are fodder for our cannons that continue to come through this suburbanism. On the battlefield you made the sovereign borders have no place. In their place, hydro geographies that tell us where the water lays. Grab a divining fork. It is a deep belonging that is unnerving and solidifying, as if neurasthenia or catatonia was a foundation for culture. You go back but not far enough, not fair enough, not half enough. In that space of ranch home, hills hoist, bungalow, the paradise that remains are seen mournfully, residue in open space, jam in a tin can. But the suburbanist knows. They know.

11

Archipelago Republic

There is a man on an island in an archipelago who dreams of the sea. In his dreaming, the sea is not the water beneath our feet but the 'plankton', 'plastic', 'stars' of language. He wants to enter it, to play and frolic, to surf, to fish for perch, herring, snapper. But he cannot, for in his dream he floats above the water, flying. He floats close to it, so close he can almost touch it, and he does get the taste of it when the waves rise high. He breathes in the sea, drinks it up even as it is salty. And, out of his mouth comes language. From the sea, the sea of his dreams, he learns how to speak. And when he wakes on his island, he goes to thank it, to kneel down and speak to it in the language it gave him, in the language the sea taught him when he was sleeping.

When he speaks to the other islanders in the language of the sea, they say he is speaking a dead man's tongue for they cannot understand him. To them, he is speaking like the devil. They avoid him but he speaks on, telling them of all the words he learnt when he was flying in his dream. They ignore him and get on with the tasks that make the suburb – farming, mining, banking. He is cast out and walks to the other side of the island, through the thickets of trees along the well-tarred roads.

He falls asleep and in his dream, the vision of a boat comes to him. It is not a large ship with sails and rigging, but a canoe built for him alone. And when he wakes he builds it even as he does not know where it will take him. The parrots seem to call to him, to ask him to venture out, to see beyond the world, and the letterboxes ask for postcards.

And the next day he sets sail.

After many sleepless nights, he comes to dream again. In his dream, he learns that he will come to an island with suburbs like his own. When he wakes the next day, sure enough he reaches the island. He starts speaking to the people on it, but they do not listen. He has no message they say, only the tongue of death.

And the next day, he sets sail.

After many sleepless nights, he comes to dream again. In this dream, he arrives at an island. When he wakes the next day, sure enough he reaches an island. He starts speaking, but they walk away. They do not welcome travellers here. There is no message they say, only the words of the dead.

And the next day, he sets sail.

He reaches another suburb on another island and one thousand and one more. And then he dreams that he will die when he reaches the next shore. He does not want to sail on, but the ocean pushes him. When he lands, he prepares himself for death. He prays to all the gods, he washes himself, he goes through the rituals that he learned from his parents. That night, he does not die but dreams of returning to his island, returning to what he knew before he left in his boat all those days before. He wakes in the morning with no one to guide him. He did not die so he does not know the truth of his dreaming. He is in a strange suburb on a strange island with manicured lawns and white cars. All he has is his canoe under his arm. But, in his field of vision, there in the morning light, he sees a parrot or an eagle or a dove or a raven or an owl. It is coming for him. He speaks with it and asks it to guide him:

'Take me home, take me all the way home.'

He arrives at the island where he has never been, an island he cannot see the end of, an island with no edge, round and fragile and blue and floating and alone in a sea black and frothy with stars and the moon. The people here greet him and his bird. They see he has come from far away, all the way from death, and in a language he recognises, they ask him to sit and speak of life to them in the suburbs then and there. And so he does.

*

He remembered watching lightning come in off the island, on his canoe, watching it flow, jagged this way, sparking with flame. The thunder rolling in, the clouds metallic-grey with that *Wetterleuchten* quickening the heart rate. From the boat, not the stoop nor the open field, watching that lightning man dance, coming in from the distance, coming down from the universe.

He had felt lightning in his life, been struck by it, laid low by it, a thunderbolt to the brain, or, the mind, heart, soul, the complete self. The sky opened up, not to swallow him whole or drown him with rain, but to show him the way.

He was there flying when lightning hit the ox cart, or was it the outrigger or was it him as he rested in yet another suburb on yet another island, as he walked from afar, when he alone saw death and the earth opened up. In that moment, he saw all is the world in its very self, presence, what it was to comprehend the moment in its eternal singularity, in its universal particular, in its luminescent hopes.

He felt lightning once more in a dream where an ancestor came to him to speak of the task at hand, what was to be done from where they stand. A person wrinkled with time carrying within themselves the ancestors of the past from all over the world, from saltwater to desert sand, from mountains to islands, from clouds of lightning to shores of contentment.

And he woke up.

Lightning came into him, into his heart, kidneys, lungs, spleen, gallbladder, appendix, thorax, pancreas. He forgot the mist and the haze and the day, as it turned into stars and he drifted on into the night, on a current of belonging. He could see the future of all life, all of it, and the death that would come for them when the time was up, when lightning ran out.

And he knew what lightning meant, knew what it was to find it in darkness, to watch and wait for the strike, for the minute of insight when the weight of the world lifted, when he saw what it was to be conscious, to become at peace, at one with the cosmos from the crayfish to the planets, from the beetle to the galaxy, from the wood to the sun. And when lightning came next, he would be there to meet him as one.

*

Weightlessness, he becomes you. You are more than contentment, more than pleasure with terror, more than satisfaction, joy and beauty. He knew you in his body and his hopes, in his dreams of rest that come on the shores he had reached. You are a blessing; a blessing of the sunset, the dying down, the peace of mind.

He has felt weightless on the slopes of volcanoes, looking down at the bay and into the ocean where he is home. He has felt that sense of belonging, not of nature in its never-ending vastness, but the harmony that comes with culture in a place where lava meets stone meets carving meets civilisation and the moon, with clouds and jaguars and all the world's visitors. Standing there, looking down upon the ruins and across the distance to the mountains, it made sense to be in the pocket of a warm earth mother's apron, to be created by the place in such a way that he was made again, not anew, but reconnected with his faith of being alone, a moment of *freedom*.

He has felt weightless flying home. In the dreams he has of navigating the world, soaring over cloud and patchwork quilt of wheat field, dusty brown and reddish hue, the scarp below and the townsfolk in the distance, greeting him with warm feeling. A homecoming when he did not know he belonged, knowing that this is out there alone, a place with all his people coming in from the edge to rest here, to relax and find comfort in those streets, to wander and reflect on what it is to come from here. That is the feeling when he flies in his dreams of language itself.

He has felt weightless in the warm embrace of his beloved, when they have sat together and laughed at what has happened, about how far they have come and what they have seen together, the days they walked through rolling green hills and the nights they spent in gatherings of culture, the time they dreamed of a quarter acre with chickens and remembered when they had come home after so long on a boat. It may yet come to pass that this is how they will go on.

He has felt weightless in the marrow of his bones, in his tongue when it was on fire, in his lungs as he swam underwater. He has known you for moments and hours, for years on end when he did not know better. He sees you every evening when he moves from one chapter to another, from one star to a million others, in the pink and orange and red and purple haze of the dying day when the night fills us with hope of what he has accomplished and how he gets to spend the rest of it, forever.

And he sat there, and the people gathered around him and cried. And their hands held his hands and they sat together. They said 'Help us map who we are and our postcodes and our flamingos, our subdivisions and our way stations, our lightning and our sunsets. Belong here, come home.'

*

This is an island in the archipelago of language, islands that together form a republic in a sea whose name we do not know but a place that when we reach it, feels like home. It is a continent that grows inside us so. This is a place that feels like we have known it all our lives, as if it was deep in our body somewhere, that it was our heart. But, it is hard to know where we are when we stand in the shallows, when we stand on the shore, wondering how we might go and find out about our home in the world as the lightning rages on and the sunset burns to charcoal.

12

From Redgate

I am back at Redgate. I am alive in Redgate. Redgate makes my body electric, atomic, cosmic. It opens me out to the world, taking the sweat from my brow to the salt water that covers the reef in the ocean, where my father and I stand pulling up craypots from the depths below. There are sharks here also; and herring and skippy, and abalone in the ledges where the tide rushes in and out. There are pippies and cockles and plovers. There is a sea eagle with a nest on the limestone cliff, and a grouper that we sometimes see when we go swimming further out. We have watched salmon run and school in this bay, and whales off in the distance moving up and down the coast when it is the right season, when the bark on the karri peels off in long strips the colour of pink and brown. The karri forest is further to the south but we have planted them on our property so they can be seen from the house. To the north, there is a café on the beach next to where they hold the surfing competition once a year. When that happens, a whole circus comes here with the world's best competing for an oversized cheque and points in a ranking system that determines who is number one. We watch them carving the water like gymnasts, acrobats milking the froth and spinning like tops for the assembled crowd. Up the way, there is a church painted white as if this place were a Greek Island, some birthplace of civilisation where they debated what a play is, how to amuse the poets, why the gods have abandoned us. But that was already happening here; always was, always will be Wardandi land.

I have been coming here all my life, or at least, since I came into consciousness. Redgate is there in myth and reality, in words and the body, in magic and logic. It can be found between the jarrah and the marri, the orchids and the grevillea, down near the grasstrees where the kangaroos are sleeping in the warmth of the day next to the granite outcrop covered with moss. I have been here in the six seasons and those in between, on days when the leaves change and the breeze switches place so that, just down the coast, the kite-surfers can play, picking up speed and getting airborne from the waves. Redgate is the place I dream of when I am away. It is the place I come back to, think through, sit down, and break bread with. It is a place where I feel like I can be my self with a true consciousness of world historic spirit regardless if death is on the shoulder to remind me that I am a guest.

I lived here for a time after I left graduate school and came back from travelling. I was working as a waiter at one of the wineries, doing yoga, and enjoying the solitude of being in the bush by myself. It was a productive time, it always is, and there were opportunities that came with living here rather than visiting for weeks, or months, at a time. The newspaper became used to my letters to the editor, the community groups found a welcome member, and the beach caught the impressions of my feet as I walked those shores each and every day. It is a place that is unique, but it reaches out to extend a hand – the water here connects us all from Little Redgate Beach to Maui, from Margaret River to the Atlantic, from Meekadarabee Falls to the Arctic. We can call it by other names. But we know, from the surfers to the swimmers, the fishermen and divers that the water needs to be cared for, with bag limits and re-vegetation schemes. It is a coastal place and we are a coastal people, and our relationship to this country involves caring for it in such a way that we know what it is to manage and protect.

Here, I have seen whales beach themselves; and national park become luxury villas for weekenders. I have seen housing developments go up on floodplains where the old people speak of wading birds that flew to a lake that was created overnight with the rains. That is in the suburbanising corridor, where the new houses with neat lawns and good fences radiate out from the centre of towns – Vasse, Dunsborough, even on our doorstep, up the road in Witchcliffe. There are new petrol stations to service new cars and new daily deals when you purchase fuel using a card from the new supermarket. You can drive through for burgers or coffee or fizzy drinks. There are fly in, fly out services for the miners who work at the other end of the state, the same blokes who could not imagine an oil rig just off the shelf down here but happily rev their jet-skis when they are on their break.

And that is one part of Redgate, but the country speaks of itself too, speaks back to our contemporary age, sometimes with a sigh, sometimes shouting as loud as can be, sometimes in a language that is subtle and full of surprise. There are people who interpret that in different ways from the traditional owners to park rangers to tourists, and poets in between. When we walk, we walk together, towards an understanding of the place and its meaning, many languages being braided by water and wanting after massacre and heartbreak.

There is a stretch of coast that I know, it runs south from Redgate to a spring and a lookout; to a cave where people have held fires and told stories. I walk along the beach, and up the ridge, through heath and scrub, on craggy limestone that cuts my feet, into head high grass, and emerge with a view that is wide open. It is a vista that extends to the horizon, uninterrupted blue, green and grey of the ocean with white waves that break off shore, and shadows that are the reefs below. The cliffs and headlands can be seen to the north, and to the south it is all beach, sand soft as flour that I can pour through my hand and see speckles of purple, orange, blue from shells pounded into dust over years. On my way there, I might see an emu or a honeyeater or a dugite stretched out, sunning itself on the path of red brown dirt. And then I think, for a moment, of what is happening inland – the wineries with their dams that have caused the water table to drop so that the stream running through this cave is dry this time of year. I think back to when I was a child and we used to catch gilgies just near the house, when you could swim in a creek on the neighbour's property, but that has receded into myth, a memory of a simpler time. It is no use missing that moment of mine, and the past is never as good as we think it was, even as we must pick through it like bowerbirds at dusk.

As nature changes, the town changes too and so do relationships. When I lived here the seasons shaped our conversations. I have watched the frenzy of summer tourism turn into a close-knit winter with fires and hibernation, less time standing round the coffee van listening to the young buskers playing folk tunes on ukuleles, and simply dashing in and out to get potatoes to mash with roast lamb. No more endless beers and burning skin, but chai and plans for Bali. When we invited people over they brought heavy shirazes with notes of currants, spices, chocolate, and we stoked the fire with jarrah logs while the rain beat down on the tin roof. And, we talk of our gardens and the possums that are getting under the nets, wreaking havoc on our crops of spinach, nasturtiums and saltbush. We speak of the soil under the fingernails and how we dwell in this one place if not settled then at least connected to the world.

We have had people visit us from all over the place – our neighbours who speak about their woodfired pizza oven and the duty free whiskey that they picked up on their last overseas trip, giving us advice about the silver princess and the family of skinks; school friends of my father who live at the other end of the Cape who come with stories of beachcombing and building, including tips on how to recycle aluminium tubing; cousins from my mother's side down from the city who are here to take photographs of surfers and spend days chasing waves, travelling down bumpy tracks in old four wheel drives; my wife's parents visiting from 'the East Coast' who burn back the bush and play cards with us (we win); friends we know from distant shores who have made the long trek and sleep the whole night with dreams of places they belong to, who we take to see where the Southern and Indian Oceans meet, imagining there is nothing in front of us but water all the way from here to Antarctica, no ships, no reef; and *yalbus* of my *gumbarli* who he knows from further north along the coast where there is iron ore.

I think of this, have thought of all this, when I have been as far away from Redgate as possible. As a child, we travelled a lot as a family, to South East Asia, India, Europe, America, Africa. But, I had it in mind from a young age that I wanted to see the 'world'. Working in a fast food franchise on my weekends during high school gave me the money to head out there. I spent a year sleeping on couches in California, New

York, Europe, Singapore, reading books, going to galleries, watching live music, undertaking a Grand Tour. And still, even if I could not say what I was missing, I knew I was missing Redgate. I remember boarding my flight home from Frankfurt with the Sydney Olympics opening ceremony playing on the television. It was curious to be going back there in a national moment such as this. It felt like I belonged to somewhere deeper and truer than a simple nation but this is what I was presented with. I was not there for the Apology to the Stolen Generation or the Vote on Marriage Equality, but Redgate is not only about an abstract if very real politics. It is its own place, my kind of paradise, my kind of utopia, my kind of heaven in the making, which has to learn how to run alongside other forms of belonging.

I left again for university, first to Canberra and then to Philadelphia, broken up with time in the Pilbara, Kimberley, Top End and Desert; and, afterwards, had stints in Berlin, Paris, New Delhi, Melbourne, Bombay, Kochi, New York. And each time, the keening grew stronger, the desire and the fantasy pulled me closer. Here one can reconcile the teachings of Anjengo and Berwick Upon Tweed, of Malayalam and English, of India and Europe, of Buddha and Jesus, of Lao Tzu and Homer, of Marx and Darwin, of life and death, of you and me – into Isaacs Rock, into Noongar, into *boodjar*, and all the others. That is possible at Redgate, in this place, on this continent, with my people, with the readers who are yet to visit these shores.

This is belonging and Redgate is somewhere the heart grows fonder for. Upon returning and returning once again, I notice new things even when they seemed to be old and known. The way the wattle blooms and the blue wrens hop, the way the surfers unzip their wetsuits, the way the backblocks have become suburbs next to vineyards when they once were farms and pastures. Redgate is not frozen in time – there is a new dosa van, the limestone pit has been dug deeper, the neighbours have changed. But the texture of life, the feeling there, the idea and spirit of a place remain a republic of poetic resonance.

It is the crayfish season now, and my father and *gumbarli* have been taking my nephew out with them in the morning. He is young and this is the first time he can walk across the reef and play in the water. It is time to pull the pots and to see what comes up, to find in them a reflection of who we are and what we see below, to find out whether we have a lunch that they would envy anywhere in the world. And Redgate, as always, provides us with that hope if not an answer to every question we might think to know.

Conclusion

I used to live on an island of my own mind in a suburb on the outskirts of philosophy and sociology and history. I was part of a community of intellectuals and artists and gardeners, but I was not connected to politics, to religion, to country, least of all to myself. As the snow fell and the drunken voices sang out and the cars passed by and the gunshots broke the night sky, I began have visions of what might come to pass. This was a dream of a home on the ocean, of where I might awaken away from this suburb. It was about home on the wave, about sailing on and waiting for the rain, for the sound of whales, and the sighting of sea birds. Here it would be about knowing that we get tomorrow, that we can keep going upon the water, that we watch and engage, that we criticise and learn. Out there, we always get tomorrow, and with that, a new dawn and a new day and a new dream, and, a chance to find new suburbs of meaning.

When I returned to Philadelphia many years later in the process of writing this book, I realised that those days had passed. The neighborhood I had lived in was in the grips of gentrification, whereas I was now interested in the retrofitting of bohemians. The city had changed as had I. I was in a sea of wealth looking at people looking for direction and kindness and mystics; for the cosmic fishes to guide them. When I looked around, when I looked back at where I had been and what I had done from this place now, I realised I was from the suburbs, and deeper still from the water, that I had a talismanic lobster leading me further backwards than I could have expected.

In past lives and this one, I was a suburbanist, but also a seafarer, a sailor, a swimmer out there on the waves with others. In India, Australia, and on Ngarluma *ngurra*, I always had eyes on saltwater even if the cars and pools and motorhomes made you glance elsewhere. If I had learnt to be a poet in these places, I had learnt to be someone from cities, towns, and countries that were by the ocean. I was from port culture even as I was trying to name the suburbs for what they were and are. This is what it meant to be open, to face outward, and not because you fear the people inland from where you stand, but because you trust that the desert can look after itself, that the mountains will too, that they will send songs to the world through you and with you no matter how far you journey and not matter if you cannot go on, alone.

The possibility is there, however, to never arrive, to never make landfall, to be safe on the waves, and return to where we come from, to travel to our home suburbs in the depth of our being, to become at peace with water when we are burnt to ash and spread there, or when our body is turned overboard, or when we slip away, drowning at dusky nightfall. But if we arrive, we are welcomed by people who came before, and that is where I belong, where mixing between old and new happens, where weary fellow travellers come to play, to trade, to exchange, to barter, to revel in the possibility of poetry and story and song and law and vision and desire and dream. To make these new suburbs worthwhile. Our role is to help others navigate that world, to speak with people, to give them compasses and maps and anchors and parrots and sails. To give them oceans and cosmos and hope. And themselves.

I understand what my role is in that place and the depth of contentment that is possible when you are open to the disciplined practices that ground you. And I saw all this when I returned to where the world meets itself, to America, which gave me a chance to see where I stood and what I had learnt since that winter in Philadelphia, since I had lived in India, since I had gone to Redgate once again. If I had come back to rescue my younger self, I also wanted to see the world be remade, not in my image but in a truer reality of its deep being. I had travelled that whole time only to come back lost, to transcend this moment through the written word and pass the message on, to see what being enlightened meant to me in the here and now, in this world, speaking truth to power with our brothers, sisters and non-binary siblings who are facing death just like we are, who want more than they find in their own suburbs, great as they are. That is what it is to be a poet with the word to carry you on. That is the way we learn to row the life raft for others and return home, to give ourselves to the world, and be swallowed by water when the time comes, and our postcodes are flooded with love.

APPENDIX

Keywords for Suburbanists

activist listening: A process of politicised close reading that comes through ear work. This is a process that is dialogic and acknowledges that the starting point for one's own practice must be a worked through understanding of one's teachers, who are everywhere, and the performative potential latent in all language games.

archipelagic republicanism: The knowledge that the continent contains within it 'countries', which approximate but are not contiguous with 'suburbs' as a type of 'island'. This republicanism, which is archipelagic and continental, is the political working towards freedom and a legal-juridical system that is a treaty *and* a universal declaration of needs.

centrist gazing: A response to the ceaseless desire to always be placed elsewhere, this is the balanced apprehension of one's location not as the sun in a universe of Others but as a body to revolve around. This may be the counterpoint to North or South or East or West yet vacuumed of their metropolitan universality and their competitive relativism.

dense clarity: The slowly apprehended discourse that nevertheless reflects a sustained enlightenment. This might be thickly fogged but once on the inside of its logic it becomes remarkably clear.

diasporic dreaming: The imaginative possibilities that are enabled through movement that is not tourism or displacement. It is an awareness of one's connection to and identification with materials outside the body.

heavy journalism: Well thought through common sense reportage that is deeply responsive and philosophically disciplined.

investigative application: Neither experiments nor instrumentalisation, but the openness of curiosity demanded by having fun with language that seeks to be read, engaged with and part of the worlds that do exist, including in their very performativity.

language puzzles: Speech acts, word texts and language artefacts that are neither rituals nor markets but indeterminate valences that heighten ambiguity even when subjected to 'activist listening' or '*mabarn* criticism'. They are texts that might approximate the canonical because the interlocutor cannot finish with them.

middling transcendentalism: The emotional experiences available in quotidian life that approximate release from worldly suffering and alienation. This is weightlessness as a temporary state, but might be available from the pleasures of a realisable style of life.

re-contextualisation: This is the structuralist, historicised version of de-familiarisation, which is to say the alteration of context rather than text in such a way that the paradigmatic environment is revolutionised.

renewed localism: The body is a territory with a history, which exists as a site of enlanguagement. From such a base one can realise that renewing the self through corporeal rituals enables one to permaculturally attend to the ecosystems one is of.

rooted connectivity: The paradoxical sense of 'deep attachment' and 'fucked networks', which is itself a response to the discourse of unsettled nomadism. It is meant here as a way to accurately describe a sense of place that does not reify fixed locations or romanticise hunter-gatherers.

seagulls: Those who like a chip off the old block. People who, out of laziness, fear, disinterest continue to feed off the leftovers of history without a dialectical care in the world for traditions beyond their comfort zone, self-interest or privilege.

splitting voter: The antithesis of the swinging voter – this is the citizen in a representative parliamentary democracy who maintains an ongoing attachment to ideology beyond the policy and media cycles. In practical terms, that means consistently voting for one party in the lower house and another in the upper.

suburbanist: A consciousness, a language and a lifestyle. The truly realised good life that is immanent to suburbia, which is to say an embodied way of thinking that synthesises the possibility of country-city in an ever expanding and becoming present and presence. Being a suburbanist involves the retrofitting of illumination with the lightning strike of the earnest larrikin.

suburbanist irony: The world is dialectical so only a homonymic consciousness can apprehend its totality. It could also be a sarcastic contronym.

superbase: The mind field between the superstructure and the base.

trilectical: A three dimensional movement, of thesis, antithesis *and* synthesis simultaneously.

Wembleyisation: A specific type of building that recycles, upcycles, songcycles the material base in a sustained and sustainable way. One might, for example, affix solar panels to an old house or re-work old poems to make them less experimental. This is the internal negation of embourgeoisment, a remaking together of French cheese that was once melted.

white ant theory: White ants have an incredible ability to eat out the insides of a structure, especially of wood, while having it appear in tact. That is to say the surface appears untouched but the guts are gone and when you touch the thing it falls over. In that way, theory as it is often performed here is like this – superficially there but without its own depth. It is there in institutional poetics that is simply faddish and referential. These are the white anters.

*

Redgating: The bulwark against the expansive sprawl of the suburbanite – of being connected to country in such a way that allows one to manifest the properties of *Geist* of that place. The following are also a subset of keywords emerging from land, which means they have simultaneous definitions that are embodied, environmental and emotional.

coal-buoying: Preparing the fire for mum so that when she gets down next time she doesn't have to set it up herself; late morning; duty and generosity; sore cheeks.

crage: When you pull a craypot and you can tell someone has pulled it before you because you are in a new moon cycle and you know they stole your crays; early morning where the light has not reached the ocean; resignation and rage; a clawed hand.

gilgied: When you go to the grog shop and run into the Witchcliffe Progress Association Committee who are just up the road but a world away; after midday before sunset during a light rain that comes in April; anxiety and excitement; small sweat on the upper lip.

gotemway: When you are fishing for herring and you see the fish come up, but it slips off the rock; on the edge of evening when the moon has risen over the dunes but there is a little light left on the ocean; like defeat but also nostalgia; a dry mouth.

long homing: The moment when you turn left from Boodjidup Rd onto Caves Rd and pass through the valley at any time of day to know that you are almost home; fog rising on a winter morning so that you can't see the bottom of the road or grass but from the car it is clear skies ahead and everything seems to float; mixture of longing and homecoming; lightheadedness.

makmer: The feel of the cold water on your feet after running through hot sand in summer or the burning of an outdoor shower in the winter rain; a rare hot day in Bunuru just before Djeran; slight shock but a numbing pleasurable one; slight pain in the lower back, near the kidneys.

mondayana: The pleasure of taking your time so that it gets done, always tomorrow; latest morning; happiness and warmth; brunch style chatter.

podogged: The noise of your own heart when you sit drinking red wine on the veranda with your wife; hail coming down on the roof; contentment and desire; light-heartedness.

rexpert: The sound of your own voice as you talk about your work; early dinnertime; arrogance and aloofness; incredulous fingerpointing.

rightide: The feeling you have when you know you have made the right decision; sunset at the rock on Redgate on New Year's Eve; welcome togetherness; laughing interrupted by high pitched squeals and long sighs.

sandboxed: When you come home from all morning at the coast and climb into bed for a nap but there is still salt and sand in your hair; peak white light, peak summer; dirty plus content; stiff unwashed hair or itchy stubble.

twightlitten: Of bringing someone here for the first time; evening sky with a heavy cloud formation that makes the light yellow but not orange or red; pleasure and fear; tight shoulders with an open chest.

uggspensive: Going to the nouveau riche holiday homes that are nearby that are ugly and expensive; a kind of inky darkness with a trace of damp; disgust and repression; a sweaty, greasy handshake. It could also just be pricey sheepskin.

Acknowledgements

Versions of these essays have been presented at conferences, work-shopped or published previously, including 'Notes of a Gumbarli' at *Active Aesthetics*; 'The Next Suburb Over' in *Sydney Review of Books*; 'Suburbanist 6014' at *Columbia University*; 'Birds of a Mirror' at *ASAL 2016* and in *Plumwood Mountain*; 'Notes of a Malayali' in *Rain Taxi Review*; 'Theory Ordinaire' in *Journal of Poetics Research*; 'Big Box Island' at *The Cappuccino Adda* at Kitab Khanna in Bombay. Thanks to their workers, editors, publishers, funders, and readers.

This book is dedicated to my parents, who continue to realise the best of a suburban life in their time, to live out their ideals with a sense of respect, affection, and generosity. Their commitment to each other and their place is something I will always look up to. Thanks for making Wembley a welcome home.

I have been thinking about the suburbs for many years now, not only while growing up in them, but also in conversation with other intellectuals. I firstly want to thank my wife Kelly Fliedner for helping me see them anew. She is kind, warm, critical, engaged, intelligent, and always helpful. Without her, this would be a shadow. We often joke that she is a Nelsonian whereas I am a suburbanist – she follows Nelson Mandela, Maggie Nelson, and Nelson from *The Simpsons,* and, to be honest, I think her way is better. I would follow her to the ends of the earth forever.

Thanks also go to the rest of my family, with whom I have shared many memorable moments in various postcodes – Sharmila, Rohana, Andrew, Taj, and Maya. You all make my suburbs a kind of utopia in which I happily dwell.

Thanks of a personal nature go to:

- Ben Etherington, who grew up across the tracks from me in Subiaco, and always welcomed me in his home. He knows how to make good nachos.
- Sam Dalgarno, who I met in Canberra, that suburban capital of suburban capitals. For your love of bus stops, for always being up for good chat, and in recognition of loving all football codes, many thanks.
- John Quattrochi, who I wrote my first poems with in America, and who shared the sense that outlet malls were a way of life that radiated from a past buried somewhere on the other side of the world. Baseball caps off to you.

Professionally speaking, I want to acknowledge Camha Pham for her help in getting this manuscript ready. To my agent Clive Newman and my publisher Nick Walker, you have both been supportive, patient, and generous. To Dennis Haskell for his erudite praise And, to a number of readers and conversationalists: Yuot Alaak, Luke Beesley, Charles Bernstein, Sampurna Chattarji, Jill Churnside, Ellie Duke, Rob Goldberg, Matt Hall, Ranjit Hoskote, Priya Kahlon, Megan Lickley, Amy Lin, Chris Lin, Leah Jing McIntosh, Sisonke Msimang, Kathy Peiss, Kevin Platt, Karl Robinson, Andrew Roff, Laurie Steed, Zaineb Syed, Iris Fan Xing. And to Jane and Jeroen den Hollander, in whose Riverstone a lot of this work was polished. Without you all, this would not be possible. We will have a sausage sizzle together!

The following organisations have also supported me: Endeavour Foundation, The Centre for Stories, PEN Perth, Columbia University, Butler Library, Copyright Agency, Tarruru, PennSound, New York Public Library; and, Department of Sport, Local Government and Creative Industries in Western Australia.

Finally, warmest thanks go to the diligent critic, the determined bookseller, and the open-minded reader. You all make the lifestyle consciousness of this poet worth embracing.

www.ingramcontent.com/pod-product-compliance
Ingram Content Group Australia Pty Ltd
76 Discovery Rd, Dandenong South VIC 3175, AU
AUHW020135130726
429791AU00003B/121